How to Sell Your Carvings
Advice From the Pros

0 11557 02798 3

How to Sell Your Carvings
Advice From the Pros

Marie Bongiovanni

STACKPOLE
BOOKS

Published by
STACKPOLE BOOKS
5067 Ritter Road
Mechanicsburg, PA 17055
www.stackpolebooks.com

Printed in the United States of America

10 9 8 7 6 5 4 3 2 1

FIRST EDITION

Cover design by Wendy Reynolds

Excerpt of "The Wild Geese" from The Country of Marriage, copyright © 1973 by
Wendell Berry, reprinted by permission of Harcourt Brace & Company.

Library of Congress Cataloging-in-Publication Data

Bongiovanni, Marie.
   How to sell your carvings: advice from the pros /
by Marie Bongiovanni. — 1st ed.
      p. cm.
   Includes bibliographical references.
   ISBN 0-8117-2798-X
   1. Wildlife wood-carving—United States—Marketing. I. Title.
NK9712.B66 1998
736'.4'688—dc21
98-5702
CIP

To Dale, for your perspective

❖ CONTENTS ❖

❖ INTRODUCTION ❖

"Whatever you can do, or dream you can, begin it. Boldness has genius, power, and magic in it."—Goethe

Have you ever met carvers who know their subjects and demonstrate an exceptional knack for carving but, for one reason or another, haven't been able to turn their pursuit into a profitable endeavor? Or less-talented individuals who through smart promotional strategies have managed to create a strong market and successfully sell their work?

Your creativity and love of the art form may have led you to carving, but an understanding of marketing principles is critical if you want your craft to generate income. Perhaps you initially pursued carving as an occasional escape from your full-time occupation but have found that it occupies more and more of your free time. Even when you're not working with wood, you may often find yourself thinking about it and wondering about the prospects of carving as more than simply a hobby. Friends and relatives may have commented on the quality of your work, and maybe you've even won a few ribbons at competitions. If so, maybe it's time to see if you can sell some of your creations.

This book is designed as a practical guide to help you decide whether carving is something that you could, or would even want to, pursue as a business on a full-time basis. Many professionals began their carving careers after a series of chance events, whereas others deliberately sought the opportunity to start their own businesses. You may recognize your aptitude and possess an entrepreneurial spirit, but you'll need to determine whether you can create a sufficient demand for your work.

This book introduces you to marketing basics, such as how to identify target markets and create a consistent marketing image.

Some of the top carvers in the world share insights gained through years of experience to help you develop a thoughtful approach to self-promotion. You'll learn about the importance of positioning yourself within the wildlife carving market and discover hints on how to develop a *differential*, a distinctive style that sets you apart from others. This book is designed to help you handle business and marketing concerns like a professional, effectively and efficiently, so that you'll be free to focus on your art as much as possible while operating a home-based business.

In some ways, being your own boss will offer the potential for more independence and more satisfaction than you might derive from any other occupational pursuit. But in other ways, your responsibilities as a full-time carver may curtail your freedom, mobility, and the amount of leisure time in your life. If you're working out of a studio in your home, you'll be physically closer to your family than if you commuted to work every morning. Yet free time with your family may be limited because of deadlines and commitments, and unlike those who work for an employer, you won't get a paid vacation. Unless you're working, you won't be making money, at least not as you begin your carving career or until you have other people working for you.

"When you're doing this for a living, you only get paid when you produce, so you have to be productive every single day," says Floyd Scholz. "You have to be a person who sets goals for yourself—daily goals and long-term goals. If you don't, you're going to be like a ship without a rudder.

"You have to work extremely hard at this, and long hours. I've been in the studio since six o'clock this morning, and I'm going to be here until ten o'clock tonight. You have to have tremendous self-discipline. You have to have drive. You have to have the desire to do your best work every single day, not as if you worked in an office where if you feel lousy one day, you might go in and say, 'Uh, I'll just shuffle papers and make it look like I'm busy.'"

The most successful carvers are those who have been driven, persistent, and sufficiently enthusiastic to sustain their vision through difficult times. Through a combination of timing, talent, determination, and for some, luck, they've turned their passion into profitable full- or part-time endeavors.

IN SEARCH OF BALANCE

In your pursuit of carving as a career, you'll need to find a balance between business and artistic concerns that is compatible with your personal and professional goals. Some talented carvers prioritize artistic considerations and pay little, if any, attention to business concerns, and they sometimes live on a shoestring. Other full-time professionals approach their art very much like a business, always eyeing the bottom line as the basis of all decisions on how to invest their time and money. And other award-winning carvers have reconciled business and artistic concerns to earn comfortable livings doing what they're passionate about.

"To a great degree, success hinges on your ability to market your work," says Pat Godin. "I suppose it could sound a bit mercenary or commercial at times when you talk about how you market your work, but the bottom line is that if you want to make a living at it, you have to sell it. You have to sell your work so that you can survive and continue carving in the future. And if that's what the market demands, you have to cater to it to a certain degree. I suppose that's just a fact of life that you have to live with, and hopefully it won't stifle creativity entirely. In the long run, the ultimate goal for those at the top of the field is to create good pieces of art."

"To achieve a balance between art and business is the biggest struggle we've had," says Dave Ahrendt, who creates carvings with his wife, Mary. "It's a struggle when you have to survive based upon carving as your sole income. It's a significant issue to anyone who wants to carve full-time, because you have to recognize that in order to survive you're going to have to spend a portion of your time marketing your work.

"Some people go into art because they like art and they want to be an artist and they want to create art. A lot of our growth and change and that type of thing has been stimulated by business decisions. We understood that somehow we had to be different than everybody else; that in and of itself was a decision based on business.

Then again, it was a business or marketing decision when we understood that our strength was in design and what related to that was studying art principles. We recognized that to get our work accepted as art was definitely in our best interests. Therefore, we moved into that area to study and to get everything that we could get our hands on to improve in those areas."

In order to devote more time to artistic concerns, some carvers delegate business concerns to a hired assistant or to a spouse who possesses financial or marketing smarts. Delegation frees the artist to be creative while someone else schedules shows, takes care of the books, and deals with gift shop and gallery owners and managers. Even if this isn't an option as you get started, it may be once you're established. In the meantime, you might decide to turn a portion of your work over to a gallery to take care of some business concerns. But you'll have to exercise at least some business skills to successfully negotiate with the person in charge of the gallery.

MARKETING = COMMUNICATION

Marketing is often perceived as a vague or obscure term. Some carvers think it means strictly sales. Some think it means promotion. And many seem to bristle when they hear the term, responding as if the notion implies deceptive advertising practices and that art and commerce must always be mutually exclusive.

But to create promotional messages, to get the word out about what you as an artist want to communicate, does not have to "contaminate" your artistic goals. If you're genuine in your approach and retain your integrity as an artist *and* a businessperson, effective communication can actually help further your artistic philosophy as well as your pragmatic goals.

In a sense, marketing involves every aspect of communication that relates to your carving. It involves everything that your work itself communicates as well as what you express through other facets of your life. And through a critical mix of variables—product, price, pathway, and promotion—it helps match what you create with what collectors and other buyers need or want.

YOUR IMAGE AND INTEGRITY

A critical element in the marketing mix, which will be explained in more detail later, involves the creation and refinement of your image. Again, this need not be a fabrication but can be authentic. Your image is simply another facet, or a sum of facets, of your self-expression and what's really unique about you.

Your image is the result of everything you do that communicates something to others. It's the total impression that you make on others and their total perception of you. It's a dynamic process rather than a static entity, insofar as it's created by the messages that you send and others' interpretations of those messages.

Through self-exploration and an understanding of some of the marketing principles in this book, you should be able to come up with an image you're comfortable with. Your image should allow you to adhere to your ethics while highlighting whatever is distinctive about your artistic style and perspective. You'll project your image through your art itself and, if you're marketing oriented, through all of your promotional communications. When you create an advertisement, for example, or put together a brochure to promote your classes, think about incorporating some of the design elements that characterize your work. If your carvings typically incorporate distinctive colors or stylistic elements, create a logo or a graphic design that conveys a similar feeling or attitude.

Get a broad overview of your marketing strategy, and develop a comprehensive approach to communications. Your image should be evident in everything you create. It should be apparent in your ads, in newsletters you send to your clientele, and even in your exhibit booth design.

If all of your promotional tools are linked together stylistically, your distinctive signature will be recognized in various contexts. For example, let's say someone recently noticed your logo, even subconsciously, on your brochure or on a business card in your booth at the Easton Waterfowl Festival. If they later thumb through the current issue of *Wildfowl Carving and Collecting* and spot your logo in an advertisement for your carving classes, they likely will recognize it.

As a carver, your specialty entails self-expression and creativity. These will be assets as you develop your promotional repertoire. Your imagination will be called into play as you design attention-getting advertisements and as you brainstorm ways to generate publicity by getting free exposure in newspapers and magazines. You'll need to find ways to "hook" an editor with a well-written news release that will make the media want to pick up your story. And if you're successful in getting coverage, you'll gain an additional advantage, as potential customers generally believe newspaper or magazine articles to be more credible sources of information than advertisements.

When you create a carving, you share your perception and understanding of the world with others. "It's very rewarding for me to take a block of wood, and through a lot of time and patience and effort, transform that block of wood into something that people will look at and be moved by," says Floyd Scholz. "You're creating something from nothing and something that affects people positively. A piece doesn't leave my studio until I'm absolutely thrilled with it, knowing that I'd like to keep it on my mantle. That's very important. When I finish a piece and deliver it, the biggest thrill for me is to see how excited my customers get.

"It's rewarding to create a lasting thing of beauty that will delight people. You're helping people to love nature a little more. When somebody's got a beautifully carved little chickadee on their countertop and they look at it every day, they may stop and look at real chickadees outside. Then they might take another step to enhance their habitat."

Effective promotional communications can help you spread your own artistic message to a broader market. If you're reticent about promoting your work, you'll share your perception and view of the world with a narrower audience. But if you express your unique perspective, *and let others know about it*, you may help someone else see the world differently—and perhaps even live in it differently.

❖ CHAPTER 1 ❖

Do You Have What It Takes?

Although there is no one profile of a full-time professional carver, research within the past decade has shown that certain characteristics are likely to lead to entrepreneurial success. Starting a home-based business takes a certain amount of vision, some chutzpa, self-discipline, and lots of hard work. Discipline, drive, and determination are also key attributes, along with strong motivation, good interpersonal and communication skills, and the ability to plan and implement strategies.

"The most important thing that I've seen again and again is dogged persistence, and I think that sort of thing grows out of really loving what you do and having it be the most important thing in your life," says Bart Walter. "If it's very important to you and if it's something that you really enjoy doing, then all the different aspects that you have to pull together to become a successful, professional artist won't seem nearly so objectionable. And even the things that you have to go through to complete a carving won't seem like work because they're fun. That's what drives a successful person in any business.

"You have to wear many different hats. You have to go to the store, and you have to be a photographer, and you have to be an editor, and you have to be a good writer of personal letters, and you have to do your own PR. It's a lot better if you can find somebody else to do it, but occasionally you get stuck writing something. And frequently you're your own secretary. And the list just goes on and on and on. You're the gofer. You're the C.E.O. You're the person who makes all the decisions, all the business decisions. You have to anticipate things before they ever take place, so it's a constant guessing game."

As your own business manager and public relations specialist, you'll need to aggressively seek publicity. If you're shy or reserved, self-promotion may be a bit of a challenge as you get started. But to market yourself effectively, you'll have to learn, at least to some extent, to blow your own horn. Ernie Muehlmatt emphasizes the importance of promoting yourself: "When I began carving, I did all kinds of stuff to publicize myself. I'm big on that. I called one of the major Philadelphia papers and asked them to come out to do a story on me. They came out and I got a whole page. Then I started doing classes, and I advertised my classes in the paper." Two decades later, Muehlmatt still tries to maintain a high profile. During the Easton Waterfowl Festival, for example, Muehlmatt sometimes seeks an opportunity to be interviewed on the local radio station while the festival is in progress.

Most full-time professionals are people who get things done. In the early years of their carving careers, they did more than simply dream of possibilities. They creatively visualized their future as full-time carvers, sometimes down to the last detail of what their daily routine might encompass. They imagined the role that their art could play in fulfilling their personal and professional goals, and they possessed the determination to translate their vision into action. They developed concrete tactics and strategies to achieve their objectives. And once their plan was in place, they moved quickly to implement specific steps to reach their goals.

A detailed picture of where you'd like to be is critical to establish your direction. But it's also important to stay flexible and open-minded so that you'll be able to respond to changes in your own situation and in the external environment as they arise. Although this book and others can offer suggestions and guidelines, there isn't a formula or a step-by-step procedure that can lead to your survival as a full-time carver. You'll have to chart your own journey if you want your business to be truly your own.

YOUR BUSINESS JOURNEY

As your style evolves, so will your business. "Instead of looking at your business as an entity, think of it as journey," says Dave Ahrendt. "As you start your business, you have to have a certain amount of independence. Look around you with your eyes open to see where you fit the best. Your business will be in its infancy and will then progress through different stages of maturity. To think of it as a journey allows for mistakes, allows for change, and accepts and recognizes that it's an evolving thing, not a stagnant entity. You have to go into it with your eyes open, and you always have to continue to reevaluate what you're doing." "As with any journey, you'll hit detours and speed bumps," adds his wife, Mary, but with focus and commitment, you'll be prepared to continue on your path.

We've taken lots of little detours in our business," says Dave. "We've tried lots of things; we've failed at lots of things. But there were one or two roads that we tried where the gate wasn't closed, so we just continued to move down those roads until it looked like that wasn't the road anymore. But you have to try many doors to see which ones are open, and it's okay to go down the wrong road for a little while, as long as you don't go too far down that wrong road."

Successful entrepreneurs tend to be risk takers, but the amount of risk you're able to assume will vary depending on your current responsibilities. "When I first started out, my children were small and I was looking for a hobby to pursue as they grew up," says Rosalyn Leach Daisey, who started carving in 1979 when she was a part-time nurse. "Somewhere along the line, I realized that if I got old and hadn't tried to see what I could do with this, I'd regret it. It was like a snowball rolling down a hill, almost outside of me. I fell into something that seemed to suit me, and I seemed to suit it. As I look back, I must have had some control."

Daisey quit her job and became a full-time carver in the early 1980s, and since then, she has been the sole provider for her daughter and herself. "I'm a great experimenter, and I love taking risks because I'm not afraid of failure. I don't think there is such a thing as failure. If you try something and it doesn't work, it doesn't mean that it failed; it just means that it's not the right procedure."

Ernie Muehlmatt has been self-employed most of his life, but before he began carving, he had never enjoyed working in his family's flower business. "My brother and I worked in the family business for about twenty years, and we both hated it," Muehlmatt says. "I got to be forty. I was married. And I was in charge of weddings. One Friday I was working in the garden center, and a woman phoned. It hit me that I'd hung her wedding order for Saturday delivery instead of Friday. We whipped up some kind of terrible mess for Friday, and we never charged her for ruining her wedding day. The next day, my brother and I quit. I took over the garden center and turned it into a carving studio and gift shop. Initially, I bought decoys at Chincoteague and sold them, along with anything connected with birds.

"At forty, I started my business. I'm sixty-eight now. I took a major risk. I said I was going to carve birds and run my little gift shop, and they thought I was crazy. So that's a late start to do what you want to do. But it was the best thing. Since I started carving, I've had more fun, made a lot of friends, got divorced, traveled more, and made more money. In the flower business, we were just about able to eke out a living. When you have your own business, everybody thinks you're rich, but that wasn't the case."

COMMITMENT IS KEY

If you decide to carve for profit instead of pleasure, your perception of your pursuit is apt to change when you do it day after day. To some extent, you'll be motivated because you'll be working for yourself, setting your own hours, and planning your own production schedule. But at times it may be tough to focus on your work, such as when your children are competing for your attention or when there's something else you'd rather be doing. And like anything you *must* do, no matter how much you usually enjoy it, carving will sometimes seem like work.

"A big thing about making a living at this is that sometimes you have to do things you don't necessarily want to do," says Floyd

Scholz. "When you do it for a hobby, if you don't feel like carving for a couple weeks, you can watch TV, play golf, or do something else. But when you're doing this for a living, and you've got deadlines for commissions that you've promised collectors, you have to do it every day, whether you feel like it or not. And it takes on a whole other light. You have to really love it. And I mean with a capital R—*Really* love it—because it could make you insane. You do your best work when you're excited about it, and if you're doing a bird that you're not terribly excited about, either you have to get yourself excited or you're going to do a lousy piece."

If you're the sole provider for your family, you'll be dealing with the added pressure of a critical bottom line, particularly if you're saddled with a mortgage, car payments, and the formidable expenses of raising a family. Almost nothing tests a marriage or other significant personal relationships like starting your own business. Successful entrepreneurs are totally committed to their professional pursuits, often to the detriment of relationships with their families and friends.

Throughout your entrepreneurial career, and perhaps even more so at its start, your art and your business must be your primary focus. Carving must almost become your sole pursuit. "To be really successful at this, you have to live this art form," says Floyd Scholz. According to Jim Sprankle, "There's no halfway. If you want to be really good at anything, you have to totally commit yourself to excellence. You can't just dabble in it. You have to totally commit yourself to living it. I hear so many people say they want to carve so badly, but when they get into it and find the degree of commitment required, they change their mind."

"If you're going to make any kind of success out of anything, you've got to work," says Ernie Muehlmatt. "Anytime you're self-employed—whether it's in the flower business, restaurant, whatever—you work eighteen hours a day, maybe longer. You've got to. People think it's easy to be self-employed. People who work for someone have it made. They get vacations, a paycheck. They can work from nine to five and then not think about it when they go home. Even today, I work from seven every morning until eleven at night. I learned to do that from my Swiss father."

CONNECTIONS ARE CRITICAL

Even if, as an artist, you prefer solitude and might like to closet yourself in your studio, you'll need to interact with people—at shows, at competitions, in galleries, within your community, and sometimes with the media. Occasionally a carver may be an eccentric recluse, but most successful carvers have learned to interact with lots of different people. Social connections will play a pivotal role in moving your creations from your shop to the buyer. And if you decide to teach carving classes as a way to supplement your income, you'll have to learn to communicate with all types of students.

"You have to go out and talk with people," says Bart Walter. "You have to be able to talk with people who live around you who may be plumbers or doctors or whatever, but you also have to be able to talk to people who are very rich and very powerful, no matter how you may feel about that. I'm quite comfortable with that, but other people spend years and sometimes decades trying to get over some stigma they have about people with lots of money. To make a snap judgment about somebody because he's rich is just as bad as making a snap judgment about somebody because he's poor. And certainly, if you're going into business for yourself and your clients are people who have expendable income, you have to be able to talk to people who have earned a good deal of money in their lives. You have to treat them fairly, and if you can't do that, you can have a tough time selling your work."

Try to be sensitive and adaptable so that you can find common ground with many people, some of whom may ultimately become your customers. Develop a genuine interest in whomever you're talking to, explore his or her interests, and learn as much as you can about his or her likes, dislikes, and preferences. Learn to listen carefully, to really hear what someone is saying, rather than what you'd expect them to say. As you improve your communication skills and, in turn, develop your empathy, you'll be better prepared to evaluate how to emphasize various promotional appeals as you target different audiences. The more you understand people and what motivates them, the easier it will be to gear your message to a particular target market's needs and interests.

Establishing a rapport with others will also help you earn their trust. Getting your collectors to trust you is critical, especially if you're selling high-priced, one-of-a-kind carvings. "There are certain people that have the ability to connect easily with other people," says Floyd Scholz. "It helps in making a living at this art form, because if people are investing that kind of money in your art, first of all they have to like you. And they have to trust you before they're going to lay down fifty or sixty grand for something. So in this art form, you need to educate them about the art before trying to close the sale. If you just pick someone off the street and say, 'I have a bird carving here that costs $30,000,' they'd look at you and say, 'What?' But once they're educated about the art form and its roots, its relevance, its significance, and the amount of work that goes into it, then they'll look at it with a much different eye. That's very important."

ASSESS YOUR ABILITY

Carvers who want to survive as full-time professionals first and foremost must have ability, says Larry Barth. "They have to have talent. They have to be producing work that is marketable, that is appealing, that is strong and competent, and that people are going to want to buy. Without that, the whole thing isn't going to go anywhere. This is a quote from my father: 'Don't confuse effort with achievement.' He and I have shared that thought many times. Most people think that if you work hard, that counts for something, and in a lot of situations it does. But in a lot of situations it doesn't. It doesn't matter whether I work hard, real hard, for six months or a year on a piece—if the piece doesn't come off, it's not worth anything."

If you feel that your talent isn't where you want it to be, or you can't accurately assess your talent, seek the input of master carvers whose work you respect. Ask for their honest opinion when you take classes. And whenever you can, request professional critiques. Your performance in competitions can also provide feedback on your style, but don't be discouraged if you don't win. Whether or not you take home a ribbon is not always an accurate assessment of your ability. "I've judged many competitions where several pieces almost equivalently could have won best of show," says Pat Godin. "Yet we're forced to make a decision that one is best, and everyone interprets it as if the piece that won best of show must be the best. It isn't necessarily that way all the time. Often there are several pieces that in their own way are equally strong."

Approach competition with a thick skin, says Greg Woodard. "To survive in this field, you need stick-to-itiveness. Sometimes you're going to win when you shouldn't have, and sometimes you're going to lose when you should've won. I see guys really getting shaken when they lose. But you have to remember that it's just the judges' opinions. It hurts. But instead of getting mad, you have to get motivated."

Developing an ability to take—even seek—criticism will contribute to your growth and evolution as an artist. "A lot of people don't know how to take criticism, and it's important," says Pati Stajcar. "Your mother will love everything about your work. But you have to do your research, your homework, and you need to be open to criticism. It will happen, and it's a good thing, because you'll learn from it. Listen to what people you respect have to say. You don't know everything. Whatever someone else can add to the knowledge you have is going to be beneficial to you. Even if they say something not relevant to the piece, they might say something relevant to a piece down the road. When I first went to the World show, I would go and get every judge I could to give me a critique. I would write down everything they said, and then go back and look at the piece to see if their critiques were valid."

TAKE STOCK OF YOUR OTHER SKILLS

Your entrepreneurial path will be smoother if you can realistically assess your strengths and weaknesses. Along with evaluating your artistic aptitude and technical skills, take a self-inventory of your other characteristics. Do you deal well with people? Can you persuade and motivate them? Can you show others what's in it for them to own your carvings? How are your problem-solving skills? Decision-making abilities? Can you analyze a situation, perceive a course of action, and move swiftly to capitalize on circumstances before the opportunity has passed? And what have you learned from your past employment and other life experiences that can help you in your own business? You'll have a greater shot at success if you can synthesize and apply what you've learned in different situations and recognize when it will be worthwhile to hire outside professional help to compensate for your weaknesses.

Although Jim Sprankle didn't set out as a young adult with the intention of pursuing carving full-time, his experiences since his late teens helped prepare him for the challenges of a carving career. At age eighteen he signed a contract with the Brooklyn Dodgers. After playing professional baseball for eleven years, he joined the staff of a bank in upstate New York and managed its public relations for seven years. He then bought his own commercial refrigeration and store fixture business, which he sold when he began carving full-time in 1976.

"It seemed like each job I had prepared me for the next level, and the combination helped me when I started carving," says Sprankle. "When I was playing baseball, no one ever taught me how to lose. So when I started to enter carving competitions, my baseball experience kept me wanting to win. The public relations part of my life taught me how to market, and that was important, because when you sell a carving, in a sense you're really selling yourself. The business that I owned also taught me about marketing and how to handle the books.

"In the sixteen years that we've been married, Patty has been very instrumental in the success of the business. She's encouraging and supportive. She also has a background in public relations, so she handles all the press releases and bios, and sets up all our ads on the computer. She does so many things, and she meets people as well as anyone. It's nice when you can work with your wife; that can be very helpful."

Another couple, Pati and Dave Stajcar, have blended their personal and professional lives to become a successful team. Pati does all of the creative work and handles the bookkeeping and taxes for the business. Along with managing the house and household finances, Dave serves as a production assistant; ordering the materials for her work in wood, bronze, and marble; pouring the waxes for the bronzes; making and assembling the bases; and "getting the big stuff in position," says Pati, pointing to a 14½-foot-high bronze eagle. "He's my other half," she adds. "He fills me out. We couldn't do what we do if we didn't work so well together."

ASSESS YOUR DESIRE

As much as they love what they do, professionals emphatically suggest that you weigh all of the costs and benefits before leaping into carving as a full-time pursuit. "Don't do this unless you've got the fire in the belly—unless you *have* to do it," says Bill Veasey. "Don't do it on a whim. Don't do it if you're mad at your boss. Only do it if you have to do this thing."

To succeed as a full-time carver, says Dan Williams, "it has to be more than just something you like to do. It has to be more than just fun. You really have to know in your heart that this is a passion for you. If this is not a passion for you, there's no way you're going to make it. I've been divorced, and I know others who have been on the brink over their artwork. It's almost got to be consuming. Success is measured different ways; if you're going to be successful financially, and if you're going to be successful with some kind of inner feeling about your artwork, it has to be a passion, and that's what it is with those of us who do it successfully. I've been doing it for twenty years, and I still look forward to getting into my shop every morning."

"I've got to work all the time," says Larry Barth. "People always say, 'Oh, you must be so patient.' But I don't consider myself patient; I consider myself determined. I decide what I want to do, and then I'm determined to accomplish that. It really isn't the same thing as patience. It's determination. Patience is what you need to get through something you don't want to do. If you're reading a great book, you don't mind that it's a big, fat, thick book. If you're enjoying yourself, that's pleasurable. And when you get to the end of the book, you're sort of sorry it's over. It didn't require patience to get all the way through that book; you were enjoying yourself. And it's the same way with what I do. I don't mind the long hours I work, because I'm enjoying what I'm doing. It's exactly what I want to be doing."

❖ CHAPTER 2 ❖

Setting Goals

The foundation of marketing includes what are typically known as the four Ps: product, price, promotion, and pathway. The variables are so closely interconnected that each of your decisions about one variable will affect all the others. For example, the way you price your carvings will influence how, where, and when you'll promote them. If you create carvings in various price ranges, your promotion should include diverse ways to reach different target audiences. And the decisions you make regarding your product—for example, whether you'll stick solely with woodcarvings or develop other product lines—will influence outlets for their distribution or pathway. Whatever approach you take, your goal will be to design a total mix of the four P's that will maximize profits and achieve your other marketing objectives.

PRODUCT

To make smart decisions regarding your offerings, strive to match what you create to the needs of the marketplace. Early on, this will entail a critical self-assessment and inventory of your skills in combination with extensive marketing research. You need to find out who your competitors are, what they're offering, and to whom. Your research should also help you identify target markets, understand their needs and interests, and discover ways to create distinctive product offerings that will make customers want to buy your carvings rather than others.

Your self-assessment and market analysis will help you answer questions such as the following: Will you carve decoys, decoratives, or both? Will you create only one-of-a-kind originals or get involved in mass production? Will you sell only mass-market originals or will you sell some of your work as the basis of reproductions? Will you focus strictly on highly detailed, realistic carvings or will you create interpretive pieces? Do you plan to work solely in wood, only creating originals, or will you explore other mediums and try casting in bronze? Has your experience prepared you to teach, write, or create videotapes?

PRICE

Pricing your work will be a challenge. It's one of the trickiest decisions facing any entrepreneur, but to an extent, you can use your competitors' prices as guidelines. Ultimately your prices will be based on how your work compares with that of other carvers, as well as on other elements in your marketing mix, such as whether galleries or other middlemen will be involved in distribution. Price will also be influenced by financial considerations, such as your costs and how much of a margin you'll need.

PROMOTION

You'll have to decide how to promote your creations. This can involve publicity, participation in shows, and other forms of promotion. Whether you decide to offer one or more products, you'll need different promotional tools to reach the various targets for each product. For example, if you decide to teach and want to promote your classes to carvers, an advertisement in *Chip Chats* or *Wildfowl Carving and Collecting* might be effective. If you want to advertise your classes to retirees, investigate the cost of advertising in regional editions of magazines or newspapers geared to a senior audience. If you're interested in promoting your carvings rather than classes, you might target potential customers by sending a news release to the editor of *Wildlife Art*, or a letter suggesting a story about yourself to the features editor of your local newspaper. The value of various forms of promotion depends on your budget and your goals. Carefully calculate the costs as you compare promotional options.

PATHWAY (DISTRIBUTION)

How will you deliver your products to your customers? If you've done a thorough job of identifying your target markets, you'll be more prepared to determine the best pathways for distributing your carvings. Analyze costs and benefits as you consider your options, which include shows, mail order, special orders, open houses, artisans' cooperatives, galleries, and other retail outlets.

If you've decided to carve a variety of products, your distribution routes may vary. They might include local gift shops and crafts shows through which you can reach the market for relatively inexpensive folk art. You might promote and sell more expensive carvings directly to collectors and through galleries catering to a high-end clientele.

Bob Guge has relied primarily on an annual open house to distribute his line of primitives. "I wholesale my primitives, or smooth birds on sticks, to a few places around the country, but I sell most of them out of my home during an open house in the fall. It's a very large portion of my income. I've built up a real good customer base locally, and rather than have people come to the house from October through Christmas to buy Christmas presents, we hold a one-day open house. I make a lot of birds, and we invite everybody to come at one time." Guge's annual open house is held the Saturday before Thanksgiving, which allows him about five weeks to fill Christmas orders.

When you carve bird species that are popular where you live, you may primarily sell those creations through gift shops and directly to customers in your area. But don't rule out retail outlets in other regions where the same species occur, and where the tourist trade creates a strong demand for related artwork. For example, if you're carving loons in Maine, find out whether you can profitably ship some of your carvings to gift shops or other retail outlets in northern Minnesota or Wisconsin, anywhere else that loons—and tourists—may be prevalent. You'll have to do some research to find the outlets and invest in some promotion. If you can't afford to personally present your work to distant retailers, try to enlist the services of an agent or someone else to convince wholesale buyers that your work will appeal to their markets. You might also consider this approach for other species with widespread distributions, such as ducks, doves, or chickadees.

YOUR BUSINESS PLAN

If you're seriously considering a career as a professional carver, one of the first things you must do is create a clear, focused mission statement. Before you formulate this statement, you should have started your marketing research and taken into account your own resources as well as the external environment, even beyond your competition. Preliminary research will help you consider your goals in relation to your assets, competition, target markets, and the current economy, events, and trends.

Map out your objectives as definitively as possible, along with a strategy to accomplish those objectives. Your overall mission statement should encompass your responses to questions such as the following: Are you realistically prepared to start out on your own? What is your purpose? What, specifically, do you want to accomplish as an artist? As a businessperson? How will you balance your artistic and business objectives? Answering these questions will help you determine whether starting your own business is right for you, from both a personal perspective and an investment viewpoint.

Once you've specified your objectives, you can translate them into a business plan. Business plans differ in degrees of complexity, and they are typically more detailed when someone is seeking outside financing to start a business. But at a minimum, your plan should include a mission statement and detailed descriptions of your target markets, products, promotional plans, and financial projections. The promotional section of your business plan should include a description of your marketing objectives, target markets or audiences, and a strategy to reach each of those markets.

Target markets can be segmented in various ways, and a popular approach relies on demographics. These are characteristics that are used to classify and categorize buyers, such as income, age, sex, education, marital status, religion, political affiliation, and zip code. As behavioral science and information technology have developed increasingly sophisticated techniques, consumers have been analyzed in more and more detail. Today buyers are classified according to their lifestyles, values, attitudes, personalities, preferences, and a host of other psychographic characteristics.

The more you're able to learn about potential customers, the more insight you'll have into what influences their buying decisions. Create a profile of a typical customer within each of your target markets and, as much as possible, analyze the customer's motivations and buying decisions. Your goal is to find the optimal promotional appeal that will motivate a buyer to purchase your products (carvings, classes, or whatever) rather than anything else competing for their dollars.

Your decisions regarding the four Ps will determine your target markets. They could include both current and potential carvers and end users—those who will ultimately own your creations. End users might include carving collectors, wildlife art aficionados, birdwatchers, wildlife enthusiasts, environmentalists, and anyone else interested in the subjects you carve. If you've decided to distribute some of your work through gift shops and galleries, you'll have to convince members of your distribution network that it's in their best interests to purchase your carvings to sell to their customers.

As you outline the marketing section of your plan, think in terms of the benefits you plan to offer different target markets. The *benefits* or *appeals* of your work may be different from the *product features* or *characteristics*, and the more fully you understand this, the more likely you are to gain a competitive marketing edge. Product features tend to be tangible and include physical specifications. Benefits, on the other hand, are sometimes product features but often are intangibles that more typically prompt someone to purchase something.

To understand this distinction, consider your own buying habits or those of your family and friends. How often have you purchased something on the basis of its emotional, rather than rational, appeal? Although your last automobile purchase may have been primarily based on specifications such as safety features and fuel economy, was there anything about the style, color, or other features of the vehicle that might have influenced your decision? Even if you pride yourself on your rational approach, isn't it conceivable that in some way, even subconsciously, your perception of the automobile was affected by a promotional appeal highlighting its potential impact on your lifestyle and image? Or its ability to somehow make you feel good?

Your most effective marketing tactics will translate tangible features into appeals that will motivate your audience to buy. "You've got to make collectors believe that you're offering something they need because you're not really," says Floyd Scholz. "You're selling them a luxury. They need to buy groceries. They don't need to buy a bird carving. The bird carving comes after the bills are all paid."

Various targets will have different needs, interests, desires, and motivations, so vary your appeals dependent upon the target market. If you're trying to persuade gallery owners to purchase a carving, you'll need to convince them that its style and design will appeal to the discriminating tastes of their affluent clientele. If you're trying to convince a collector to invest in your work, you'll need to convey your credibility and to demonstrate that, because your work has consistently gained in value since you began carving, its purchase will translate into profit for the collector.

To some extent, emotions dictate everyone's lifestyle and consumption habits. Emotions influence the clothes people buy, the music they listen to, and the art they surround themselves with. A carving can speak to or move someone for reasons that they can't always identify. For example, when a customer purchases a pair of doves you've carved, they might be seeking serenity. Or when someone buys a carved falcon or an eagle, it may reflect their own desire for power, status, or prestige. The more your art portrays the essence of the species or reflects your own emotions, the more likely it will be to elicit an emotional response within the viewer.

STAY FLEXIBLE

A firm statement of specific objectives in your business plan will help you decide how to spend your time and allocate other resources. But since you won't be tied to the constraints and rigidity of a corporate agenda, you'll be free to respond to changing market conditions and to take advantage of unforeseen market opportunities.

Dan Williams has been tuned in to the photography business for more than thirty years. After shooting countless rolls of film and spending thousands of dollars to create reference photographs for his own carvings, he discovered that other carvers were interested in his photos. An astute businessman, Williams perceived the market potential for his photography and began shooting photographs for wildlife magazines all over the world. Ever since, photography has played a key role in Williams's home-based business, and today he splits his time between carving, photography, writing, teaching, and other related pursuits.

As you and your business mature, flexibility can also help you discover new markets. Phil Galatas created strictly original work for fifteen years. In 1994 he got involved with Wild Wings, Inc., a Minnesota-based publisher of limited-edition prints and distributor of wildlife art. Wild Wings purchases original carvings from Galatas and makes arrangements with a manufacturer to have them reproduced in a resin-type casting material. Galatas paints the master reproductions and after the birds are manufactured, they're hand-painted at the factory and distributed by Wild Wings to galleries throughout the country.

"I'm signing the pieces, and they're paying me a percentage to use my name," says Galatas. "Carvers often think, as I thought in the mid-1980s when I didn't want to do reproductions, that these pieces will be out there, their names will be on them, and others won't paint them like they would. The fact is, you don't want others to paint them like you would. Somebody else is making a replica of your bird. You're gearing the work to a certain market—people who are spending $150 to $200, rather than $14,000 to $16,000—so you have a whole new market.

"Ten years ago, I wouldn't have considered doing reproductions, but you've got to be thinking about retirement. I'm getting older. I can't just be doing originals. When I see a talented young carver selling high-priced one-of-a-kind originals to support his family, I ask him, 'What happens when you can't do this anymore?' Your eyes will get bad, your shoulders will go out, your neck will start killing you. You don't lose your creativity, but the work becomes physically a problem just from sitting in one posture for so long. You can't continuously work on that finer and finer detail. In order to get all the detail right, your whole back, arms, and neck are tensed up, but you don't feel the effects of that tension until years later. The reality of working at this as a living, eight to ten hours a day for twenty years, is that it does take its toll."

Galatas says that he also started doing reproductions because Wild Wings offers an avenue to increase the exposure of his work. "It's a name thing—it gets your name all over the country. I'm able to get the detail out there without having to make the same bird over and over. My degree in commercial art is finally paying off, because the instructors often told us that if you don't get it out there, nobody sees it. It used to be that you could go to a show or competition and most of the collectors would be there, but that's not the way it is today. Those days are gone for a while. You have to be flexible; if you're not, you're going down. If you have one product that's not selling, you'd better be willing to make another product.

"I'm doing plenty of original work. The income from these reproductions just fills in the gaps. It's also a good feeling knowing that I could die tomorrow and there will still be royalties coming to my family."

DIVERSIFY

"If you're going to be successful at this, you need to realize that bird carving alone is not enough to be your livelihood," says Dan Williams. "It's the same for anybody in any field of art, whether it's carving, sculpture, painting, or drawing. In this business as a bird carver—and it's happened to me—you can have years where you've got a six-figure income, and the next year you qualify for food stamps. It doesn't take but a couple of those years before you decide, hey, I'd better get something else going here. Or you quit. That's what happens to a lot of these guys: They bail out because they don't have other sources of income. So you have to be involved in a lot of different things, not just for the money, but to keep your sanity."

As you plan your overall marketing strategy and outline your marketing mix, consider the benefits of diversification. You can broaden your market in many ways. Depending on your skills and objectives, you might alter your style for different targets, vary the species you carve, or experiment with working with bronze or

marble as well as with wood. For many carvers, diversification creates a variety of income streams that are helpful, even critical, to
their survival. If there should be a slump in carving sales or a major
commission suddenly falls through, other facets of the business can
pick up the slack.

In the mid-1980s, after Pat Godin had established his name by
repeatedly winning the World Championship, he and his wife, Jes-
sica, developed their own product line, Godin Art Inc., and started
selling a variety of products, including castings, instructional videotapes, pattern books, and brushes with Pat's name on them. More
than fifteen years later, those products continue to generate revenue.

"The other side of our business serves as a buffer when I'm not
selling carvings," says Godin. "With carvings, you don't have a
steady cash flow. After a show, you might go three to four months
without cash. If you just do carvings that you spend one, two, three,
or more months on, your paycheck isn't coming in very frequently. I
do a lot of carvings that take me two or three days, or a week, and
they're ready to go. When you have other products, they provide a
steady cash flow, and you're able to operate like somebody who gets
a paycheck every week."

Godin recommends that you try to cater to a diverse market as
you're establishing yourself in the carving world. "If you're doing one
thing only, you're selling to a select group of collectors," he says. "If you
do some decoys, some songbirds, and once in a while a bird of prey,
you're not only enhancing your skills, you're broadening your market.
If you're too specific and the market weakens, you're in a bit of trouble.

"Diversify the market that you're catering to with your original
work. I've established a good market in three or four directions.
I'm not catering to a small, limited market. I'm selling stuff to different people. I'm selling high-end decoratives to some collectors,
high-priced as well as high-level artistically, and I'm also selling gunning decoys—work that's at the other end—to other collectors.
They're very simple carvings and are also at the low end pricewise.
It's important to be able to sell at that end because you have a much
broader market there. You have a lot more people that can afford to

spend $1,000 to $2,000, and a smaller number that can afford or would want to spend $30,000 to $40,000."

Another advantage of selling to a broader market is the flexibility that diversity provides when it comes to establishing terms of payment for your work. If you've successfully tapped into different markets and you're selling both lower-priced and higher-priced work (even though it may not yet be as high-priced as that of the top pros), you'll be less reliant on income from a commissioned piece that may take you months to complete. As a result, you may be able to offer the option of manageable payments over time to a collector who might not otherwise be able to afford your work or who would rather not pay the full amount up front.

"Right from the beginning, I didn't think that I was too good to do real simple, cheap things like little silhouettes cut out on a dowel that I sold for a few dollars," says Bob Guge. "I started to do the more expensive, detailed pieces right away, but I also did other kinds of things, including my primitives. It paid my bills, and it paid for my table at a show. And through the shows, I met a lot of customers and a lot of collectors. There were a lot of people that couldn't afford a bird for a couple hundred dollars, but they could afford $2 or $3 for a little silhouette that was handmade. And through that, I built a good customer base locally.

"I do a lot of primitives, smooth birds on sticks, and I capture the essence of the bird with as little work as possible. They go anywhere from wholesale $25 and up, and they provide a big portion of my income. Think about the market. Out of a thousand people, you might have one that can afford a detailed bird but five hundred that can afford one of these primitives. But I didn't do it because of the sales; I did it because I liked it. It's kind of my sketching, my loose work. I don't have to look at anything; I can do it the way I want. It's fun. And it's quick."

Although you may eventually want to specialize in intricate, time-consuming works of art such as those that win World Championships, that approach may not be realistic, artistically or economically, until you've been carving for a while. If you produce some carvings relatively quickly, you'll be able to charge less, sell more, and appeal to a broader market. At the same time, you can work on more challenging carvings that will bring a good price and show collectors what you're capable of producing. This strategy will help you establish a solid financial base for your business as you're building your reputation and a clientele to commission you to do more expensive work.

You can also broaden your market by learning how to carve species with wide popular appeal, such as hummingbirds or shorebirds. These can be fairly simple, not necessarily primitive, but not terribly delicate works. "To select your subject matter, ask yourself what sells," says Dan Williams. "I can sell ten cardinals for every mockingbird. Pick up *Southwest Art* magazine or one of the wildlife magazines, and look at what some of the painters are selling."

Some sculptors enjoy working in various mediums while also gaining the financial advantage of limited editions. Although carving wood remains Leo Osborne's primary focus, he occasionally creates a bronze sculpture using clay or wax as his original. He now also molds some of his burl wood originals and casts them in bronze.

"It helps me survive, because I'm not as dependent upon having to do one-of-a-kind pieces," says Osborne. "It also allows me to have more gallery representation, simply because of the number of works available—between twenty and thirty bronze images for each original. And it allows people to acquire bronzes for less money than a wooden original might be, although certain people want the uniqueness of that one-of-a-kind piece. Others simply like bronze more than wood.

"The tough part is that it's extremely expensive. For example, an eight-foot eagle cost $3,000 to cast, plus another $3,000 to make that mold. So to get the first piece done, I'm out $6,000. And they sell for $15,000. If I'm selling it to a gallery and they take anywhere from a third to half of that $15,000, I'm barely making my money back on that first one that sells. So there's a big investment of time and money to produce bronzes. One of the nice advantages of casting from my original burl wood piece is that at least I also have that to show and sell, whereas a clay or wax original is just recycled when you're done with it.

"My passion lies in the burls. The real passion I feel when the work is completed is more evident in the burl wood originals than in anything else. They're just so sensual. Touching that finished burl wood sculpture, there's a real energy about it that people can feel and are really drawn to."

Given the expenses involved in working with a foundry and casting in bronze, you'll have to weigh the costs and benefits of this option in relation to your individual style, resources, and goals. A number of highly respected sculptors have successfully created superior work when casting from their wood originals, but others have been disappointed by the financial or artistic outcome when they have tried this approach.

Some professionals have discovered other drawbacks in diversification. After strictly carving birds out of wood for most of his professional life, Larry Barth decided to explore other avenues. "It seemed like I had all my eggs in one basket, so a number of years ago I started reviving the various mediums that I had worked my way through until I had gotten to wood," he says. "I started to view clay as an end product in and of itself, rather than just a means to the end in wood. And I started working in clay as a finished medium, and that made it a very natural jump to bronze.

"But as soon as I started doing all that, I started feeling too strung out, as if I'd lost my focus, so currently I'm back in wood. I had my spell of exploration and experimentation, and I enjoyed it thoroughly but found it frustrating at the same time. I'm still working in clay, but I found it too difficult to try to market the clay to a clientele that was familiar with what I do in wood. I wanted to do all those things because I felt that wood was limiting, but now, having done all those things, wood seems so comforting and simple. So I'm back to working in wood and quite happy doing so."

Your artistic style, self-assessment, and insights into the way you work should help you define the parameters of your own business. Your willingness to experiment and take risks will influence your artistic growth and the evolution of your business. With experience, you'll increase your understanding of your creative process and develop a more specific answer to the question: "What business am

I in—or do I *want* to be in?" Even though the boundaries of your enterprise should stay flexible so that you can respond to new market opportunities, a definitive answer to this question will help you retain your focus and know when to say no.

Diversification may offer psychological benefits as well as financial, if you don't enjoy spending most of your time by yourself. For one thing, you'll be forced to vary your daily routine and may not sit still carving by yourself day after day. "It takes a special personality to work alone every day, day after day," says Jim Sprankle. "I love it, but some people can't do it." Today Sprankle also recognizes the benefits of a multifaceted business. Although he spends about two-thirds of his time carving, his business is structured into three different categories: carvings, seminars, and mail order, through which he sells such things as videotapes, brushes, and study casts. The mail-order operation is handled primarily by his wife, Patty, who also handles most of the arrangements for Jim's teaching seminars.

TEACHING

Teaching may interest you and seem like a good way to supplement the income from the sale of your carvings. But it will require time and commitment, and time spent teaching will be time away from your solitude and creative side. Students will take as much of your time as you will allow. And if most of your classes are on the road, they'll involve time away from home.

Some believe that there's less demand for carving classes and teachers than there used to be. "Ten years ago, you could hang out your shingle as a carving teacher and fill up your classes," says Dan Williams. "Teaching can be very lucrative. If you charge $600 per student and get ten of those students for a week, that's $6,000 a week. So the money's terrific. Ten years ago, all of us were teaching. I had fifteen classes, ten students apiece, and the whole class was full. That's a lot of income from teaching. But it's not the case today." Despite extensive and expensive advertising, some classes reportedly have failed to reach even minimal enrollment.

Yet teaching continues to be profitable and rewarding for many professionals. It's not necessarily an option for everyone, though. You need to establish a name for yourself before you're likely to fill your classes. To some extent, your teaching prospects will be influenced by where you live and the market you're after. "You have to command some kind of respect to create an initial following to do your classes. The teachers that do a good job get their students to come back," says Jim Sprankle.

Before you commit any time or money to teaching, do some market research to determine whether you could get a class off the ground. Try to assess whether you have what it takes to be a good teacher. "You can be a great carver and not be a good teacher," says Sprankle. "To be a good teacher, it takes patience and an ability to encourage people. You really have to watch people and see that they're getting it down. Some may need a little extra attention."

"If you have a good name, you can command a good price to teach," says Pat Godin. "What kind of name you build influences almost everything you do. If someone has reasonable skills, you might not make lots of money to start with, but you can build a clientele and make some money teaching. It just supplements your income over the long term. But you have to be careful about not pricing yourself out of the market for your classes. In a lot of cases, you're dealing with people who have a limited amount of funds.

"About seven or eight years ago, I realized I was doing so much teaching that it was interfering with my carving. But that doesn't mean it isn't good money. If I wanted to, I could have made $30,000 to $50,000 a year just teaching. The time I used to spend teaching, I now spend sitting and carving. From a creative point of view, I get more satisfaction out of carving than I do out of teaching. But I wouldn't discourage anyone from teaching. It's a good supplemental source of income."

Some master carvers taught for a while and became frustrated by some students' lack of willingness to take risks or to create anything original. They feel that teaching took away from their carving time but did not prove to be a satisfying experience in return. Other experts, on the other hand, are happy about what teaching has done for their carving and feel that it improved their productivity. Some say that it enhanced their style by leading them to carve a broader range of species.

CHAPTER 3

Finding Your Niche

MARKETING RESEARCH

An increasingly complex and competitive marketplace makes research more important than ever. With some creativity and resourcefulness, you should be able to conduct marketing research with minimal expense and learn as much as you can about potential markets.

Your research should offer insights into your competition. Exactly who are your competitors? Are they strictly carvers, other craftspersons, artists? Are they local, regional, national? What are they offering? To whom? At what prices? Can you identify their differentials or distinctive selling points?

And what about your customers? Who appear to be your best prospects? Where are your target markets? What does your research reveal about their demographics? What are your targets' needs and interests? Likes and dislikes? What newspapers and magazines do they read? Do you know anything about their other media viewing habits?

Based on the details you've gathered about your competition, can you identify any needs among your target markets that are not being met? What can you offer to satisfy those needs? What are your strengths and weaknesses compared with those of your competition? What will you emphasize in your marketing to capitalize on those strengths? Will you highlight your style? Quality? Selection? Price? How can you position yourself within the marketplace to optimize your competitive advantage?

Libraries and good librarians are often underutilized resources that can provide you with valuable marketing research data. Get to know your local reference librarian and explain, as specifically as possible, what you're seeking. (Having met the librarian will also be an advantage down the road when you're ready to arrange a one-person carving show at the library.) Ask him or her for market studies or census reports of your area. Try to find local clubs or organizations interested in the subjects you carve—for example, hikers, bird-watchers, animal lovers, or wildlife enthusiasts. Find out if the organization publishes membership mailing lists, which can come in handy when you're seeking targets for promotional mailings or catalog and brochure distribution. A well-trained librarian will also offer hints on additional sources for you to search on your own, such as CD-ROM, on-line databases, and World Wide Web sites.

In addition to researching the markets, investigate how other entrepreneurs have successfully started their own businesses. At shows or competitions, seek out self-employed carvers and ask if they'd be willing to share some of their experiences. Some carvers are reluctant to discuss business, but most seem open to questions and will help those just getting started. The pros are often busy at competitions, between judging and dealing with their own clientele, but they might be able to spare a little time to talk with you. Or introduce yourself and ask if you could arrange for a telephone meeting at a time that would be mutually convenient.

ON-LINE MARKETING RESEARCH

Given the growth of information technology and the development of the Internet and the World Wide Web, it's a lot easier and cheaper to gather marketing research information today than it was a decade, or even a year, ago. On-line resources for carvers are proliferating, and more and more carvers around the world are networking to share hints on marketing and new techniques. The Net and the Web can help you learn about trends in the marketplace, new tools that can help a novice gain a competitive advantage, and ways other carvers are using computer technologies to help their carving and their business.

If you haven't yet discovered these resources, your first stop might be the Woodcarver Mailing List, which allows carvers to correspond daily with everyone on the list. The list was established by Bill Judt, who is also the editor and publisher of *WWWoodc@arver E-zine*, a bimonthly publication dedicated to promoting woodcarving on-line. You can locate the list and E-Zine by searching the Net with the help of Lycos, AltaVista, or another search engine.

You can also keep up with trends in the carving world by subscribing to magazines such as *Chip Chats* and *Wildfowl Carving and Collecting*. But don't limit your browsing to carving magazines. Also check out what's covered in magazines that deal with wildlife and related issues, such as wildlife art magazines, and find out what is being discussed in newspapers and magazines geared to the market for art, as well as arts and crafts in general. Read the letters to the editor in addition to the articles.

Your research will be more comprehensive if you pay critical attention to what's going on around you. Scan your environment for marketing-related information as you read your daily newspaper, browse in local gift shops, and surf the World Wide Web. And stay abreast of current events by regularly reading your local newspaper and at least one weekly newsmagazine. Your heightened awareness will help you anticipate trends, which can be instrumental in the growth of your business. Sustained marketing research may also ultimately impact your marketing mix by familiarizing you with new distribution options created by new technologies or by suggesting new themes for your work. For example, your awareness of significant environmental issues or the identification of a newly endangered species might lead you to carve what prove to be highly marketable subjects.

COMPETITIONS AND SHOWS

As you wander around a carving competition or a wildlife carving or art show, observe the crowd. Try to get a sense of the attendees' demographics. Talk to carvers. Talk to collectors. Talk to casual customers. And pay attention to what show visitors are saying to each other. If it's a selling show, observe what the customers are buying. Evaluate the response to other artists' work. Notice what seems to be selling and how what's selling is displayed and promoted. If you're exhibiting at the show, analyze individuals' response to your work. If someone inquires about something that's not on your table, note their inquiry and consider whether it might be worth producing.

Also pay attention to what sells at general art shows and crafts shows. Try to determine how buyers at general art shows or crafts shows differ from those at wildlife art shows such as the Easton Waterfowl Festival. Compare audiences and analyze the differences in demographics as much as possible. Ask whoever is managing the show to provide some insights into the types of people who frequent a particular event. If you're considering participating in a particular show, attend the show as a visitor a year in advance to decide whether it seems worth the time and money to participate. As you scout out the show, talk to exhibitors and get some feedback on the selling prospects.

DEVELOPING A DIFFERENTIAL

Developing a *differential*, whether it's real or perceived, is key to marketing success. To understand this concept, think about the work of well-known carvers. When you see one of their birds, you often know immediately whose work it is. You recognize a distinctive quality that characterizes that particular carver's work. It's that distinction, a certain "signature," that sets their work off from others and constitutes the differential.

If you've seen Dave and Mary Ahrendt's award-winning work at shows or in magazines, you've noted their innovative approach to carving. But their distinctive style wasn't an accident; it was the result of a conscious effort to be different. Before the development of their style, according to Mary, the couple "didn't know exactly what the style would end up being."

"One of the most challenging things we've done in our career has been just to achieve our own style," Dave explains. "When a person makes up his mind that he's going to be different and not do what everybody else is doing, that's the key to developing his own style. But it doesn't just happen. You need to make a conscious decision, and you need other influences. You must understand the technical side but must also be stimulated by design and apply it so that you come up with a style of your own.

"When we started, our focus was not on art, but on making a living. It was basically a cottage industry that was focused on producing bird carvings for the purpose of making a living. We started at a time when there weren't a lot of bird carvers. Our birds were not very good, but they were inexpensive, and we were able to sell them and make enough to live on. We sold them through some wildlife art galleries in Minnesota and also did local shows. We went from carving ducks to carving songbirds to carving different types of birds that seemed to be selling better.

"At some point in time, we understood as a business that there were so many people starting to do this, that in order to survive, our work somehow needed to be different than other people's work. There needed to be some reason that people would want to buy our work other than the fact that it looked like a real bird. So we started to experiment and to study art principles and design.

"We realized in analyzing our strengths and our weaknesses that within this realistic bird-carving community, we didn't know anatomy as well as other people. Therefore, we knew that we couldn't compete where the criterion was that the bird had to be perfect; our skills weren't ever going to be good enough for that. But we'd had encouragement regarding the design of some of our realistic pieces, so we tended to focus on our strength. We continued to pursue the artistic end of it and continued to study art and art principles."

Rather than limiting themselves to the study of sculpture, Dave and Mary methodically set out to study design by analyzing "anything visual that had an element of design in it." They studied principles of design in landscape, architecture, pottery, painting, and bonsai. The couple's intense period of study, combined with their strong desire to be different, led them to create carvings that integrate an impressionistic use of natural wood with minimal paint and realistic focal points. By sculpting works of art that are notably different than others' and that can't be classified as strictly realistic or as strictly impressionistic, the Ahrendts created their own niche. "When those pieces started to first get shown, about four years from when we commenced, then everything changed dramatically. Then it was a new game, so to speak," adds Dave.

As you design your marketing mix, try to create your own niche. Think about strategically *positioning* your carvings so that customers will perceive them as satisfying previously unfulfilled needs. Positioning is based on how customers perceive your work compared with that of your competition. Your positioning strategy can highlight product features, benefits, your image, or a combination of the three. If you position yourself as a high-quality carver, all of the elements in your mix should be in sync: You should be doing quality work, charging a high price, distributing your work through high-end gift shops and galleries, and promoting your image in classy media. Once you've successfully positioned yourself, you should be prepared to maintain your position. "I've seen carvers fail miserably because they got a lot of orders and just started cranking them out," says Jim Sprankle. "They just started to beat these birds out," and their quality suffered.

To determine your niche, compare yourself with your competition. Consider what other carvers are offering and what they're charging. Given the insights into the marketplace that your research has revealed, think about what you can offer that will be superior to and more expensive than the others, comparable and less expensive, or somehow different.

Some professionals seem to have found their niche without even trying. "I think your art tends to reflect your personality," says Jett Brunet. "My dad has always done birds larger than life, more colorful, a bird that's sure to be noticed. His work has always stood out from the crowd, as he does. As an artist, you have to separate yourself from the crowd. Compared with everyone else, the Cajuns are just a little different. Our unique way of living, our certain flair for living is maybe what's reflected in our art."

REGIONAL DISTINCTIONS

Just as a particular design distinguishes a quilt as Amish or a piece of redware pottery as Pennsylvania German, there are distinctive regional trends in carving. There are contemporary carvers along Maryland's Eastern Shore who create decoys in the tradition of the market gunners, and carvers along coastal North Carolina who pattern their work after the crude but functional carvings of their ancestors. Some of the simplest and least time-consuming carvings are associated with traditions. And you can create a niche based upon regional traditions, styles, or subjects, drawing on these distinctions to enhance your work. This can be particularly effective if you're trying to appeal to the folk art market.

If you live in an area where certain species of birds or other wildlife prevail, think about incorporating these subjects into your carving. Carving what appears around you may help you tap into a strong regional market for your work, as well as enrich the quality of your life. "Just being able to see your subject every day should help you become so familiar with it that you can do it well," says Pati Stajcar, whose sculptures include elk, eagles, magpies, and other birds and animals that are abundant near her home in the foothills of the Colorado Rockies.

Jim and Patty Sprankle were surprised to discover a distinct regional market when they moved to Sanibel Island, Florida, in 1994. "When I lived on the Eastern Shore or in upstate New York, for the first twenty-four years of my carving career, all I was focused on was waterfowl because I was living in an area where interest in waterfowl was so great. When we moved to Sanibel Island, it took us about six months to realize that the market down here wasn't going to be for waterfowl. We discovered that we couldn't sell ducks in Florida—we couldn't even give them away! We also had a difficult time filling up the carving classes.

"We realized that I'd have to carve something else to earn a living down here. So I started to carve wading birds—herons, egrets, and avocets. I'm fascinated with herons and egrets because that's what I see every day. They're around our house and around our swimming pool. I can put these birds in so many positions in my carvings, and they're so graceful. And I'm glad that I had this new situation to refresh me, to get me charged up again. I'm so fascinated to see these birds. I never realized that I could be happy carving something other than ducks. I wouldn't have guessed that the market is so regional."

You can also combine regional tradition with other lore. Leo Osborne, a native of Maine who now lives in the Pacific Northwest, is also highly influenced by his environment. Osborne moved to the Pacific Northwest in 1989, first to the mountains of Oregon and then to the San Juan Islands in Washington.

"Out here we still see native people who continue in their ritualistic societies," Osborne says. "The creative arts of those cultures remain very strong and dominant, even today, particularly in woodcarving. The Northwest natives were tremendous woodcarvers, and the carvers were very important to the tribes. Some of them were shamans. They had great wood to work with, and they used it in many of their ceremonies, from smoking fish to creating masks and canoes and totems and all sorts of wonderful carvings.

"So for me, being basically a woodcarver, that's pretty inspiring. There's a spiritual energy here. You can feel it running through the thread of the people. A lot of the wood sculptors who work here are also inspired by the early vision and the early visionaries. And some of the carvers here today have taken some of the early wildlife subjects, like the wolves, the fish, and the ravens, and extended them into their own personal vision."

One of the first carvings that Osborne created after he moved to Oregon was a fairly large piece in burl wood titled *Brothers in the Wood*. The piece tells a story about the symbiosis between the raven and the wolf. When collectors buy art, they're sometimes seeking a conversation piece, so a good narrative to accompany the art may enhance its appeal.

As the story goes, a raven is often seen flying in the direction of where there might be a possible kill for the wolf. "The wolf will follow the raven to help him find food," Osborne relates. "So then the wolf goes in and does the kill, and then he feeds. Once he's done, he goes off and sleeps. Meanwhile, the raven comes in and dines on the remainder of the carcass. You'd think that would be the end of it; that's pretty neat symbiosis in itself. But then, the raven sometimes will hop over to the wolf and jump around it, taunting the wolf, and the wolf will lunge out lazily with his paw, and they have this lazy exchange that I call the dance of the wolf and the raven.

"These two creatures are quite different in nature, but through whatever means—whether through simple survival or through the spiritual energy that also runs through animals—they've learned to live together in a unique harmony. They have allowed this symbiosis to take place, to shape their lives. I find it metaphorical of what humanity is slowly learning to do. We're gradually being forced to learn the dance of the wolf and the raven."

❖ CHAPTER 4 ❖

Refining Your Style

SEMINARS

Before you sign up for a seminar, try to assess your skill level, your needs, and the style to which you aspire. Identify your goals in taking a class. Some classes focus on painting, some on bird anatomy, and some on the use of tools or other facets of carving. Are you interested in songbirds? Wading birds? Birds of prey? Would you like to improve your painting skills? A particular texturing technique? Do you feel that you already have a good grip on techniques and need to learn more about bird anatomy? Are you seeking step-by-step instruction based on a pattern, or would you like to pursue your own design under the guidance of an instructor?

Professionals have different approaches to teaching. An instructor's teaching style is influenced, to some degree, by his or her distinctive carving style and philosophy. Some instructors focus more on the details of the process than on the outcome or artistic effect. So before you decide on a class, do some research. Investigate the instructor's style and credentials. With your goals in mind, phone or fax the instructor to ask questions. What will be covered in the class? How much will the class cost? How will the class be run? For how many days? Will class size be limited? Has the instructor taught this course or a similar course before? How many times? Will tools be provided or do you have to supply your own? If you have to supply your own, how much will they cost? Can the instructor provide the names of former students as references?

Although the professional may be well respected, you should still seek the opinions of one or two former students. Someone can be a renowned carver but lack the patience or communication ability that makes a good teacher. "Do a little research to find out some background on the instructor," advises Leo Osborne. "Is the person a reproduction artist or a real creative soul? That's part of the process of determining who to work with. It's like any apprenticeship—you have to seek out the direction that you feel you want. In a lot of the carving workshops—painting workshops too, but I find it more so in carving—people come in and are shown a model, and then they copy it. They duplicate someone else's carving. They haven't learned anything. They haven't gotten into their own creative soul and dug something out. If you want to simply be a person who does reproductions, then that's fine, you'll learn technique. You'll learn how to carve. You'll learn how to use the tools. You'll learn how to paint. You'll learn how to do all that, but you'll never create a thing. That's where it becomes real personal. Do you want to be a creative artist? If you do, then you'd better be real careful about how you pick and choose who's going to be teaching you."

Find out whether the class will be geared to novices or students with some carving experience. You want to be challenged, but not so challenged that you'll be frustrated and quit. "If you're just starting out, before blindly taking classes, make sure you know what it is that you want to do," says Jo Craemer. "What species? What style? Go to at least three classes with different instructors. This will free you up from the fear that there's only one right way to do it. What one instructor says you should never do, another will say the opposite. But it's the final result that's important."

If you live in an isolated rural area and can't find a class nearby, investigate seminars offered in conjunction with shows and competitions. Check the listings and advertisements in *Wildfowl Carving and Collecting* to find out who will be offering classes, when and where. Request seminar schedules from competition and show management.

Find out if the master carver you most admire plans to teach a course somewhere. "It should be somebody who can take you to the level that you want to go to," says Jim Sprankle. "That's the nice thing about this art form—you can take it to whatever level you want. No one says you have to compete, no one says you have to paint the bird."

Until you can get to a workshop, ask around to see if there's a talented local woodcarver or sculptor who might be willing to help you with technical and stylistic concerns. Or if you can't find a local expert, organize a group of carvers who are interested in hosting a seminar where you live, and pay for a professional to come to you.

"I think it's a principle of life that if you can work with an experienced professional in an apprenticeship of sorts for a short period of time, you're going to learn so much more than stumbling around on your own," says Leo Osborne. "When I was carving wooden signs, which was part of what got me into sculpting, I wanted to do some gold leaf work. Well, I bought a book on gold leaf, and I did all the little tests and samples and this and that. And it was very confusing to me. It was hard, very difficult. Then I found an old-timer who had been doing gold leaf for years, and he said to come over on Saturday morning and he'd show me some techniques. I spent two hours with him and learned more than I had in two weeks through reading and experimenting."

REFERENCE MATERIALS

Perhaps you don't have access to an expert or a seminar but want to learn more about carving. Although carving reference books were relatively rare twenty years ago, a significant number have since been published, and they're available at shows, in bookstores, and through catalogs. If you've decided to invest in a computer, you'll have access to on-line resources. Jo Craemer finds her computer invaluable for locating reference materials for her carvings and the carving-related articles she writes. "When I needed to find out the length of the wing for a male ruby-throated hummingbird, I accessed a search engine and typed in "hummingbird." I was referred to an interest group for bird-watching, and I asked my question, adding,

'Does anybody know a reference or the answer?' I gave my E-mail address, and when I checked back ten minutes later, I had my answer. Almost anything I want I can find on the Internet, or I can find somebody who can tell me what I need or where I can find it.

"The Internet has been a real nice tool. I live in a remote area and nobody around me is particularly interested in carving or what I'm doing, so it gives me a sense of community. It's like being able to invite a group of carvers to come and sit on your back porch twenty-four hours a day. There's always somebody available, twenty-four hours a day, that you can talk to about carving."

Whether you're doing traditional or on-line research, look for more than simply carving-related references. "Even when I was headlong into bird carving, I didn't just look at *Wildfowl Carving and Collecting* magazine," says Bart Walter, who has since moved into sculpting bronze. "I looked at *Art and Antiques*. I went to the library and got out art books on Van Gogh and Monet. Monet has always been one of my favorites, so I'd look at everything I could get my hands on that had a Monet image in it. I've always enjoyed Rodin's work, so I've read quite a few books on Rodin as well. I think it's foolish to limit yourself to the world of bird carving if you're a bird carver, or to the world of bronze sculpture if you're a bronze sculptor. You want your influences from as broad a field as possible."

Expand your artistic influences; don't limit yourself to the study of woodcarving. Consider signing up for a sketching or drawing class at a local high school or college, again keeping in mind the importance of the instructor's credentials. You can also refine your carving style by participation in summer workshops in drawing, painting, sculpting in clay, or other arts at schools such as the Loveland Academy of Fine Arts in Loveland, Colorado, and Scottsdale Artists' School in Scottsdale, Arizona.

YOUR PERSONAL STYLE

"Probably the best way to develop a style of your own is to learn to draw well. At least the best that you can," says Bart Walter. "You don't have to make pretty pictures—you're not trying to produce finished drawings here. You just need to train your eye to be an observer. And through training your eye, you'll develop a way of seeing, and that will translate through to your work. You have to put a little bit of yourself into each one of your sculptures if you're going to develop a style. It's more about being true to yourself, and the way you see the world around you, and what you want to say about the world around you, than it is about anything else."

Other top professionals also emphasize the importance of learning to see, *really* see, and they recommend drawing as a way to enhance your perception and improve your observational skills. By enhancing your perception, you'll improve your ability to convey the essence of the species.

"Sketching helps you strengthen your visual acuity," says Larry Barth. "You can sit there and observe something for a very long time, and then when you go to draw it, you find out what you haven't seen yet. Sketching is a means of exercising your eye-hand coordination. The actual sketch sometimes comes out looking nice, sometimes not, but it's the act of sketching that's really valuable, because it forces you to look at your subject in a way you otherwise wouldn't."

Barth sets out to capture the essence of the species in every carving. "When it comes right down to it, art is all about perception. An artist spends his time seeing, observing, perceiving. I go out and observe what to me is most exciting and beautiful, which happens to be birds and the things that go with them, and I get so excited that I have to come back to my studio to try to create what I've seen. But it all starts with seeing, with perception."

Along with enhancing your artistic style, capturing the essence of the species will heighten the appeal of your carvings. If you incorporate the unique way that you see the world into something with universal appeal, viewers will recognize in your work the distinctive characteristics of the birds that they see around them. And your fresh perspective on familiar facets of their environment may prompt a purchase.

"You can capture the essence of a bird, if you know what that is, in a little silhouette piece of wood," says Bob Guge. "It doesn't have to be a high-ticket product. It can be a little $5 silhouette. But you have to do a good job. You've got to go out and spend as much time watching the birds as you do making them. That's the most important thing in marketing: Know your subject.

"Your most important tool is bird-watching. It doesn't matter how well you can carve feathers, if you don't know what the bird looks like, you can't capture the essence of that bird. So if you're going to carve a chickadee, go spend a few days watching chickadees so that the rest of your life you'll have that mental image of what a chickadee looks like. Consciously, you may not know all the unique little important things that make it a chickadee, but down inside your mind somewhere, you do. Even a simple carving that captures that essence lets the viewer know it's a chickadee."

Larry Barth emphasizes that there's a prerequisite level of technical skill you must attain before you can adroitly capture the essence of a species. "The technical skills are what make you an artist rather than just an observant person," he says. "If you have technical skills, you combine them with your ability to see and your observations, as well as your feelings and emotions, to create something. If it's something that other people are interested in, they might buy it. You have to have some handle on technical skills, the craftsmanship in creating art.

"Every artist goes through an evolution. There's a set pathway that you go down, and people go down it at different speeds. Once you master the techniques, you start trying to do more and more accurate birds. You try to carve and paint better and better birds. And once you're carving and painting more and more accurate birds, then you want to go beyond accuracy and start making birds that not only are scientifically accurate but also have that spark of life. That's when you get into intangible, difficult-to-define aspects. And then you start moving into the higher planes of carving, where you start trying to create pieces of sculpture, with artistry as the final frontier.

"Those stages are in order, but it's not a linear order. It's like a pyramid. The first thing has to be achieved before you can go to the next level, and you can't succeed on any one level without having already laid the foundation of the previous level."

The whole key to success as a carver is to be unique, says Jett Brunet. "I can teach anyone to burn or paint a decoy, but to create a work of art, you have the ability or you don't. You can make a nice decoy, but to make a living at this, you have to present to the public a work of art they can't see everywhere. The most important thing is to be unique and original and develop your own personal style. You can learn how to burn, you can learn how to paint, but to become great, you have to have your own ideas. Your work has to be unique and special and have a certain style to it.

"You need constant new ideas flowing through your head. I can be working on one bird and keep getting new ideas of what I want to do for the next few years. Those fresh, new ideas are what make you successful—coming up with original ideas and visualizing. I have a clear picture of the bird I'm working on before I even start. The birds that are most successful are the ones that come closest to what I've visualized."

Bob Guge emphasizes the importance of going beyond copying others' work. "When I first started carving, I started going to some shows. There were a few individuals whose work I liked, and of course, I emulated them. But what helped my style the most was when I realized that I really wanted to go somewhere else. When I got to where I thought I wanted to be, I realized it wasn't where I wanted to be, so I changed. I went with what I felt and not with what people said I should do, and that helped me tremendously.

"Early on, I started with patterns, just like everyone else. When I started deviating from the patterns, it was the best thing that ever happened to me. It's like coloring in a coloring book—you know, you're told not to go out of the lines. Well, I started carving from what I remembered and what was in the back of my mind, and it was really a more fulfilling kind of thing. It was my bird and not somebody else's, and it was the way I saw it, not the way somebody else did. I didn't care about getting it right as much as doing it the way I felt it or saw it. And sometimes that had to do with very subtle things, such as putting more personality into the face, enhancing the bird rather than trying to make it accurate. That helped me more than anything else, and I felt like a whole burden was lifted when I did it."

KNOW THE BIRD

It's important to study the live bird and really get to know it. You can't carve a good bird unless you know what it looks like. And you need to look carefully to see what it *really* looks like, not what you *expect* it to look like. To take advantage of bird-watching opportunities, consider keeping a pair of binoculars in your car or always on hand. "I almost always have a camera with me, as well as binoculars," says Rosalyn Leach Daisey. "I need to buy binoculars like other people buy calculators—one for my purse, one for the car, one for my office. I never go anywhere without them."

Emphasizing the importance of accuracy, Greg Woodard says, "The most important thing is knowing the material, getting good study reference. You can talk about techniques and how tight the lines are, but what's important is knowing the bird. You have to get a study skin and a live bird. You have to do all the legwork. You can't just get one picture and carve a bird from it. Look at the pattern, but get the reference material too. The biggest mistake I see, especially in competitions, is that some entrants don't know how the bird works. They may be only looking at a study skin, when they should also be looking at the live bird.

"Not knowing the bird is the most common mistake novices make. I've seen guys who have been taking classes year after year, and their birds aren't getting any better. Some of them keep doing the same bird the same way. If you're doing a bird, you need to spend some time studying it. Don't just dive into the carving before you do the necessary research. And get good photo reference, whether it's actual photographs or some nice pictures that you can find in plenty of reference materials. You can check measurements by looking at pictures."

In addition to watching the birds in the wild, one of the best ways to familiarize yourself with them is to volunteer at a local nature or raptor center. As a volunteer, you may be able to touch, handle, observe, and come to understand the bird's behavior and anatomy. "Nothing substitutes for going and looking at a living, breathing bird in any given species that you're trying to portray," says Floyd Scholz. "I don't just say this; I live it. I had a big commission back in the early eighties to do a whole series of puffins. So one summer I volunteered with the Audubon Society and the puffin project, and I spent most of the summer living on the islands off the coast of Maine monitoring Atlantic puffins. I got to actually live with these birds and watch them day to day. I watched them feeding and preening and going through their day-to-day struggle for existence, and this all translated into a much more powerful, dynamic sculpture than I would have been able to do if I'd just opened up some books and looked at some pictures."

Whether it's in the woods, up on cliffs, or out on islands, go into the natural habitat of whatever species interests you and spend some time there. Watch the birds in the wild and get a feeling for why those particular birds look the way they do, why they live where they do, and how their evolutionary adaptations have enabled them to survive.

SKETCHES AND CLAY MODELS

Preliminary sketches and clay models play a key role in the artistic process for many professionals, who use them in different ways. "I'll do quick thumbnail studies in clay as well as pencil drawings to get my general composition," Leo Osborne says, "and I find that it's really important before doing a big sculpture to have a small clay study that's not too detailed—not too definitive. I like to use it just to keep in mind a purpose rather than a plan."

Jett Brunet recommends pencil sketching the bird and then transferring what you see in your sketches into clay. "Before you start with wood, understand the anatomy of that bird," he says. "That's how I'm teaching my seven-year-old son. I have him making birds out of clay. By sculpting the bird in clay, you'll get a feel for the shape, the form, the profile of that bird. Once you know the way a bird is shaped, the way it's formed, it's easier to translate it into wood. It can be very difficult to carve a decoy out of wood without having a clear idea of its form and shape. The best way is to first sketch and sculpt with clay."

Before beginning her sculptures in wood, bronze, and marble, Pati Stajcar starts with sketches of abstract lines and forms, then progresses to a series of "sketches" in clay. "I might do fifteen of these sketches," she says. "Sometimes the anatomy won't work, but eventually I'll get to the point where I can start a sculpture. A lot of times I'll find something I like in two different sketches. So that I don't lose those different aspects, I integrate them into a later version. It's kind of a growth rather than being limited to the first idea. It opens up the possibilities. That's the idea—you want to open yourself up to everything."

Says Larry Barth, "I do a clay model before every single wood sculpture, but I recognize that some people don't need to. It depends on your working methods. I'm fairly deliberate and methodical in my approach, so I need that clay model for every single project I do. Even if it's a tiny little songbird that seems to be just sitting there, with no complications at all, I still make a clay model and do all my decision-making in clay, where I have total freedom to make changes. You don't have that freedom in wood. In wood, you're dealing with a subtractive process only, whereas in clay it can be subtractive or additive. And that back and forth gives you the freedom to act boldly and do whatever you want in clay. I have the freedom in clay to make changes, and things occur to me that would never occur to me in wood. I work with the clay until I'm happy with what I've got, and then that clay model serves as my pattern. It's a three-dimensional pattern, and I go from it to wood.

"I've found that the extra time spent on the clay model actually saves time in the long run, over the life of the project. It eliminates all the time that I'd spend holding the wooden bird, staring at it, trying to visualize what to take off and what it's going to look like if I take it off, and if it's going to be okay. I just transfer dimensions from the clay model to the wood block and can cut right to the line. I don't have to creep up on it, wondering if I'm on the right track. It saves me a ton of time even on a small bird."

DESIGN AND COMPOSITION
Master carvers repeatedly emphasize the importance of design and composition. Along with your study of the live bird and techniques, an understanding of basic artistic principles will help you develop your distinctive style.

The late John Scheeler's work combined the elements that are vital to good art, says Floyd Scholz. "His birds had design. They had balance. They had beautiful color harmonies. They were anatomically accurate. They pulsed with life. John's birds all captured the essence of the species. They weren't wooden taxidermy—they were alive. All of his work told a story. That's very important, but it's sadly lacking nowadays. There's a story behind every one of his birds.

"Scheeler's carving of a goshawk and a crow is one of the most famous bird carvings ever. It won the World Championship in 1979. It's a dynamic struggle of life and death in which a vicious, intense goshawk has just killed a crow. Crows are very wily and smart, and don't succumb easily to predators, and yet. . . . The piece moves the viewer and makes you feel that you could read it like a book."

A more recent carving by Greg Woodard, entitled *Get Off My Cloud* (1997), also tells a story. It depicts the antagonistic dynamics between a red-tailed hawk and a kestrel. The red-tail seems to be sitting there minding its own business, but the kestrel, which doesn't like other birds of prey, clearly doesn't want a bigger bird in its territory.

Woodard says he designed the carving "to stop your eye, pull you into the red-tail's eyes and, with that branch, to keep you spinning. When I'm designing a piece, sometimes a line in the design will jump out at me. It could be any kind of line, in the base or the tail or a wing, and then I'll design the piece around that. Different pieces have different types of lines, but this is more about flowing. There are fast lines and slow lines, and some are sharper angles."

According to Pati Stajcar, "A big mistake in carving is that people start out with a bird, then they go out and look for a piece of wood to put it on, rather than starting out with a wonderful piece of wood they might have found. They often forgo the total design, but that's what others feel when they look at a carving—they feel the flow of the piece, the strength, the motion. Most of the time carvers forget that part because they're focused on the technical aspects and getting the feathers just right.

"The viewer's eye should just keep wanting to move over the piece and come back to the middle. It should be very balanced. And you should strive to make the viewer think. Let the viewer's imagination get involved and participate in the narrative, or it will be a boring piece."

❖ CHAPTER 5 ❖

Promoting Yourself

Y ou don't necessarily have to spend a lot of money on promotion to achieve marketing success. In fact, some of the most successful full-time carvers began with limited promotional budgets and instead relied on and developed their natural orientation toward the market. They were sensitive to the needs and dynamics of their target markets and from the start recognized the key role of communication in their entrepreneurial careers.

You need to develop and promote a *total image* to position yourself in relation to local, regional, and national markets. As you enhance your own market-oriented awareness and attitude, remember that everything about you contributes to that image. As an artist, you may care very much about your distinctive style and putting your signature on your work. From a marketing perspective, you'll want that differential to be evident in all of your communications.

Your carvings and written promotional communications will obviously affect your image, but so will things such as your phone message, the way you dress, how you interact with people, whether you complete commissions on time, and even whether you're on time for an appointment. All of these factors are important. It might be only one subtle aspect of your image that catches a collector's attention and makes him or her want to learn more about your work.

Some artists contend that as a professional carver, a creative person, you're not expected to conform to typical business constraints.

They suggest that the boundaries of how you dress or wear your hair in business situations are a little looser than they are for someone in a conventional occupation. Nevertheless, some top carvers believe it's important to take a more conservative approach to dressing for success.

"You have to meet collectors on their terms," says Floyd Scholz. "If they're wealthy businessmen and they wear suits, and they invite you to their office, take a shower, wear a suit, get a haircut, and present yourself on their level. If they invite you to their home to come over and relax in their living room, dress appropriately. Get rid of the ponytail and the earrings and the scruffy Birkenstock look, and look like a professional if you expect to get the kind of money that you want to get. I see so many artists who say, 'I don't care, man. I'm an artist. I'm me.' But if you're wearing earrings, a long ponytail, and a torn shirt, how can a collector take you seriously?"

BE AGGRESSIVE

Success is often a matter of talent, timing, and luck, and successful carvers repeatedly emphasize that if your work is good, it will speak for itself. If your carving is exceptional, and you're lucky, your success may largely hinge on word-of-mouth advertising and referrals. But it's best to supplement this with other forms of promotion.

You need to budget funds for printing and mailing promotional materials such as brochures, but more than money, you need to be creative, resourceful, and aggressive when it comes to self-promotion. You want to get as much exposure as you can get, and in lots of different places. And the more creative you are and the more angles you pursue, the more apt you are to get free coverage. "You have to put yourself out front all the time, always promoting yourself," says Bill Veasey. "You have to get yourself out there and get known if you want to make a living. Anything you can do to promote yourself helps increase the price of your work."

Develop a variety of promotional communications to publicize carvings, classes, and other product lines. A catchy business card will be an advertisement in itself, but don't get carried away with anything too cute or too clever. You can design your own logo with desktop-publishing software. You can also use this software to create newsletters for your clientele, brochures to publicize your classes or other product lines, announcements of open houses and one-person shows, and flyers or price lists if you need them in a hurry for a local show you've decided to participate in at the last minute. Depending on the range of your work, you might also need to publish a catalog.

If you don't have desktop-publishing capabilities, hire or barter with a graphic artist or someone at the local print shop to design a standard brochure. Its basic format should include a description of your style, a photograph or two of your work, and a bit of biographical detail relevant to your art. (Be sure to mention your most prestigious awards). Include your address, phone and fax numbers, E-mail address, home page URL, and so on to make it as easy as possible for customers to reach you. If appropriate, leave space (possibly the back flap) for variable copy, so that each year or season you can change your schedule of classes or list of prices.

All of your printed promotional literature should project an image that's consistent with your positioning strategy and should feature your logo or an element characteristic of your designs. Your materials should be neatly designed and easy to read—clear, concise, well written, grammatically correct, free of typos, and informative but not cluttered.

Promotional materials can be fairly inexpensive if you stick with simple but classy stock (or rustic stock, depending on your image). Before you have your materials printed, ask local businesspeople for recommendations, and shop around for a reasonably priced printer.

You may already have a home page on the Net; if not, you might wish to seriously consider one. The field of electronic communications is changing so rapidly that by the time this book is published, capabilities will exceed those listed here. But even a basic Web site can be used to display images of your art, list prices, solicit ideas, take orders, post notices of interest to collectors and gallery directors, and display a schedule of upcoming shows where you will have a booth.

You might also investigate the possibility of establishing a computerized link with related associations. For example, let's say that you carve a specialized style of decoy featured in a regional museum or you're very active in the local chapter of Ducks Unlimited. If someone taps into the museum's or the local DU's home page, with just a click, they could be directed to your home page. If you lack computer expertise, you can hire an expert to design your home page and update you on the latest ways that the Internet can help promote your business.

TARGET YOUR MESSAGES

Your entire promotional strategy should be based on targeting your message to segmented markets. Targeting should influence all of your decisions, from ad media selection to show selection and scheduling. Vary the forms of your promotional literature, and highlight different facets of your work depending on the target audience. Know your audience, and gear your message accordingly. High-powered collectors may be more interested in seeing the number of ribbons you've won or whether you've exhibited in prestigious shows such as the Leigh Yawkey Woodson Art Museum's Birds in Art, whereas casual buyers at a crafts show or those at general art shows might be intrigued by the folk art or regional aspects of your style.

The audience at some shows will be more interested in your artist's statement than in your biographical profile, and vice versa. The more you know about the demographics of show attendees, the easier it will be to select the right materials to have on hand. Your artist's statement should highlight the artistic aspects of your life rather than your overall background. You might describe the early influences on your work, how your art has evolved, why you work with wood or any other mediums, and the impact of your regional landscape on your work. "Also include an indication of your philosophy and what your mind is all about," says Leo Osborne. "Some people just list their awards, but there are many appreciators of fine art who want to know where the art is coming from. They want to know where its essence is in the soul. If it's really fine art, that's where it's coming from. That's where the philosophy comes in."

Developing a promotional repertoire will also prepare you for when a gallery director requests an artist's statement or the curator of an upcoming exhibition asks you to fax a biographical profile. You'll also be able to provide a journalist with a variety of promotional literature prior to a scheduled interview. Receiving materials in advance will help the reporter prepare focused questions and avoid asking questions that might have been answered beforehand in your literature. Your foresight should also help the journalist gain insights into your art and therefore probably write a better article about you.

CREATE A QUALITY PORTFOLIO

Your portfolio may be the only representation of your art and experience that a gallery director or exhibit curator initially sees, so it must demonstrate professionalism as well as your distinctive artistic style. It should portray the same degree of quality that characterizes your work.

The elements of portfolios vary, but in general, they focus on the art-related aspects of your background rather than on your broad biographical profile and employment history. A portfolio typically includes the following items:

- Detailed résumé
  - —Solo exhibitions
  - —Group exhibitions
  - —Selected private and public collections
  - —Art reviews
  - —Articles, videos, and programs
  - —Awards
  - —Commissions
  - —Education
  - —Seminars and workshops
- Artist's statement—a little about your philosophy and how you approach art
- High-quality photos (at least 8 by 10 inches), with specifications and retail prices
- Glossy excerpts of magazine articles about you

PHOTOS AND SLIDES

You'll improve your chances of getting free publicity if you can provide the media with high-quality photographs or transparencies.

Perhaps someone in your family is a good photographer. If not, you might learn to use a 35mm camera or hire a professional photographer.

Depending on the preference of the newspaper or magazine, you'll need to submit good, glossy black-and-white photos or color transparencies. Call the editor to determine the preferred format for illustrations. Try to submit dynamic pictures, in both horizontal and vertical formats, that relate to the information in your news release. Don't simply submit static images of a carving or two. Instead, come up with a couple of dynamic shots to accompany pictures of your carvings. Interest the editor with an illustration of you at work doing whatever it is that you do, such as a colorful close-up of you painting a carving or an action shot of you in the field sketching with binoculars around your neck.

Newspaper and magazine editors often think in terms of the play they're going to give a story—how they'll run the text and images to complement each other, and where the article will appear in the publication. If the images you submit simplify the editor's job, you're more likely to get the coverage you're seeking. And if your news release really piques the editor's interest, he or she may dispatch a reporter or a photographer for additional shots.

Pat Godin says, "One thing I've always done, for as long as I can remember, is to keep a really good portfolio of my work including photographs. It's a great thing to be able to show people. Unfortunately, with our one-of-a-kind work, we don't get to keep it. Once you let a piece go to a collector, you don't have access to it anymore, and you can't get it back to photograph. It may cost you a little bit of money to have a great photographer record your work, but it pays off in the long run. People don't want to spend the money because they can't foresee that they might need the photographs at some time. But a lot of times a magazine will call and say that they're running an article and need some photographs. I've got high-quality 4-by-5-inch transparencies of the work I've done going back fifteen or so years, and I can just fire them off—I don't have to waste time digging around looking, only to find that I don't have any. You should have that material ready to go if somebody asks for it."

High-quality photographs will do more than simply help you get media coverage—they can also be critical in terms of helping you get your work into galleries and exhibitions. For example, Eldridge Arnold is convinced that good photographs contributed to the Bruce Museum's invitation for him to exhibit in his first one-man show at the Greenwich, Connecticut, museum. While in art school and throughout his previous career in commercial art and graphic design, Arnold learned the importance of cataloging his work. When the museum contacted him, he was able to provide professional 4-by-5-inch transparencies of his work from very early on. "If you're going to take up this business and do it seriously, you should really strive to have good photos of all of your work," he says. "From the very beginning, you should photograph each piece you do to keep a record of it so that you know where it went, who's got it, and how much they paid for it."

Quality photography can also help you break into prestigious juried shows such as Leigh Yawkey Woodson Art Museum's annual Birds in Art exhibition in Wausau, Wisconsin. Birds in Art and other juried shows receive applications from all over the world, so it's not feasible for juries to review all of the works of art in person. As a result, the judging process often relies primarily on images, and some excellent artists may be screened out if they submit mediocre or poor-quality slides.

Robert Kret, director of the Leigh Yawkey Woodson Art Museum from 1993 to 1998, says he doesn't think that there's a magic formula for artists to have their work accepted into the annual Birds in Art exhibition, but it's important that they have quality photographs of their work. "The jury reviews anywhere between a thousand and twelve hundred images. Our selection process involves projecting those transparencies onto the screen. Not all artists take the time to submit high-level transparencies, and I think that first and foremost, they need to realize the importance of submitting quality slides.

"They also need to be true to their work. They should, as artists, submit work that they feel strongly about, rather than what they think the museum is likely to include. We change the makeup of the jury every year, so the complexion of each jury is different. It would be inappropriate to look at a catalog and assume that just because a certain artist painted or sculpted a particular way and was accepted into the show, someone else should follow that style in hopes of getting accepted. The artists need to be true to themselves and do work that inspires them."

THE SHOW CIRCUIT

When you're starting out, one of the best ways to make a name for yourself is to participate in shows, exhibitions, and competitions. Familiarize yourself with national, regional, and local shows, both within and beyond the world of wildlife carving. Depending on the market you're after, you may decide to put more or less of your resources into carving shows, local art shows, crafts shows, or other types of wildlife art shows that are profitable outlets for your work.

Shows provide good opportunities for you to display your talents, and they can be effective in terms of generating word-of-mouth advertising via referrals from satisfied customers. They can also be great places to meet gallery owners and managers, collectors, and individuals who might organize classes for you to teach after you've established a name for yourself.

In general, shows can be divided into selling shows and competitive shows, but the distinction isn't black and white. The following list is designed to familiarize you with the show circuit, but this is by no means a formal classification.

- Carving competitions. Shows where entries are judged, winners are selected, and prizes are awarded. Entry rules and judging procedures vary. If you're going to enter, make sure you're thoroughly familiar with the rules, and follow them.
- Juried exhibitions. Relatively exclusive shows where participation is typically determined by a jury whose composition generally varies from year to year.
- Shows. Carving, wildlife art, art or craft shows, or shows designed primarily for selling purposes.
- One-person shows or exhibitions.

SHOW SELECTION

Some carvers seem to think that if they show up at the World and at one or two other carving competitions or shows, they're getting exposure. To an extent, that's true, but it's limited primarily to an audience of carvers and others in the field. Rather than restricting your promotional efforts to a narrow segment, think about broadening your exposure and your market. Get your name and your work out there, in front of potential customers who are relatively unfamiliar with the realm of carving.

"If you just go to the World and maybe Easton, and never go to a show in another part of the country, you're really limiting the clientele you're exposing yourself to," says Pat Godin. "It may be an expense, but it can make a difference in the long run. You need to diversify your exposure to different types of clientele."

Investigate some of the more prestigious juried art shows and learn the qualifications for application and entry. When planning your show schedule, don't think only in terms of carving or wildlife art shows, where everyone is selling something similar to what you're selling. Instead, branch out into other forums, such as crafts shows or mixed-media art shows.

Assess each show in terms of how closely the crowd it attracts matches your target audience. Your criteria for selecting the shows at which you'll exhibit will vary, depending on the stage you're at in your career. "If you're just getting started and trying to get your name out there, it would probably be good to do almost anything local," says Bart Walter, "just to get your name out there and get your feet wet. It's called paying your dues. It's an unfortunate part of going into any business, but there it is. You pretty much have to see what's out there and where your market might be, and the only way to really find that is to use the shotgun approach."

"I still think the best thing for people to do is to start locally, with the little shows," says Bob Guge. "If you're just getting started, a bird show may be one of the worst places to sell birds, because everybody else there is selling birds too. But the bird shows draw the big buyers, and if you're a good carver, they'll buy from you. It can help one person, and hurt another."

Never underestimate the value of local shows; sometimes they'll lead to one or two commissions you might otherwise have missed. "Exposure is important," says Bob Guge. "Early on, I did a few local art fairs and things, and that gave me a reputation right here in my home territory, which brought me sales. I've had people who have followed my career but never bought anything suddenly come to me and say, 'I've been watching you since you were twenty years old, and we'd like to have a bird.' And it was because they saw it at an art show, or in the paper, or wherever. So you've got to get out. People have to see your stuff somehow."

The size of a particular show is not necessarily a reflection of the attendees' buying power. As you're setting your show schedule, consider small, exclusive shows that may not necessarily have a high profile but that may attract an upscale crowd, particularly if some of your collectors will be there. Do a little research and check with your local librarian to find sources of demographics for various geographic regions.

"There are some collectors who don't like to go to large exhibitions," says Bart Walter. "They don't want to stand in line for half an hour to get to see an exhibition, and they don't want to be elbow to elbow with other people. And some of these people are insulted at the idea of paying $100 or $200 to get a benefactor's badge to walk in early. So they just don't go to the big shows.

"If you have a bit of a following, a bit of a reputation, then you want to try to be more selective. Try to choose the shows that are the most prestigious for the sort of work you do. Different shows have a reputation for a stronger running in different categories. If you're doing slick gunning decoys, for instance, it wouldn't do you a whole lot of good to go to a show that's mostly known for fancy, large, decorative bird carvings. It would make much more sense for you to go to a lesser-known show that specializes in slick gunning decoys or one that is prestigious in that field."

"The Ward Show and the Easton show both have a special part in this wildlife equation," says Jim Sprankle. "They both have their particular identities. One is a competition and one is an exhibit, and I think that you need both. If you've started carving, one of the quickest ways to become known in this art form is to compete. If you're competing, you're constantly trying to do something better, but it curtails your creativity because you're always doing lifelike birds. The Easton show gives you the opportunity to develop creativity."

COMPETITION

To improve your visibility and gain recognition, consider competing on local, regional, and national levels. You can find a sampling of competitions throughout the United States and Canada in each issue of *Wildfowl Carving and Collecting*. You'll also find a selected list of events at the end of this book. The Ward Foundation World Championship is the largest competition, and if you've never been to this annual event, it may be worth the trip. This competition is held each April in Ocean City, Maryland, and winning the World has helped many carvers establish themselves as professionals and expand their collector base. Although there reportedly has been a decline in participation over the past decade, it's still perceived as the top competitive carving arena in this country, and probably the world.

On your first visit to the Ocean City Convention Center, you may be surprised by the degree of technical detail and artistic expression that some carvers achieve. If you're competing, the scene may be a bit overwhelming, and watching the judges move from table to table may heighten your anxiety. Yet it's important to keep the event and its relative significance in perspective. Yes, it's great if you win and get that recognition, but blue ribbons will not make or break your ability to succeed as a professional. Some professional woodcarvers have established successful careers for themselves without ever having entered the competitive circuit. Others see it as a necessary evil. And many say that today it plays a less critical role in a carver's chances for success than it did about a decade ago.

"I used to think that you needed to win the World Championship in Ocean City to be able make a real good living at this, but it's absolutely not true," says Floyd Scholz. "I've never won a World Championship, and I make a lot of money at this. I earn well into six figures annually carving birds for a living. I don't know many other carvers who can lay claim to that kind of success, so I'm fairly proud of that. But the best I've ever done in Ocean City was second in the World back in '92. I've been down there since '85 in the World category, so it's been sort of frustrating.

"Competition is important to a point. If you're an unknown carver and you want to improve your work and get recognition among your carving peers, competitive shows are important because they give you the exposure that would ordinarily be unavailable. They give you exposure to the public and to the other carvers. It gets people talking about you and your work. Competition also tends to make you improve. You want to win, so you work harder. And you try to do even better work every year."

According to Dan Williams, "Twenty years ago, competing was a major thing. When I first started out, in the mid-seventies, I was really big into competition. At that time, the only way collectors recognized you was if you were competing. That was the way to make your name and reputation. I traveled around to every competition in the country, and those early days of competition gave me name recognition, which was important. And in those days, when you won blue ribbons, it resulted in sales. But I would emphasize that I don't think that's the case today. I don't think competition has anything to do with sales today."

To some extent, your decision on whether to compete will depend on your goals and the stage you're at in your carving career. Winning local and regional competitions can help you develop smaller markets, but some experts claim that you'll need to win the World in order to gain national recognition. "Some collectors place a great deal of emphasis on whether that carving they're buying has won a blue ribbon in a competition," says Pat Godin. "That's unfortunate, because there are some great pieces of art that for one reason or another the judges haven't selected. A carving that has a ribbon on it may not even be as good as another carving that doesn't have a ribbon on it."

If you are extraordinarily talented, have already discovered a market for your work, and are not necessarily interested in getting national recognition, then competition may not be a necessity. "If you just want to sell birds, I don't think competition is necessary, because most of your customers don't come from the shows; they're not carvers," says Bob Guge. "Competition can help your reputation, and you do meet some buyers at shows, but take my primitives as a good example—I've never entered a primitive in a show, and I can do as many of them as I want."

But participation in the World Championship can help you gain additional exposure and conduct marketing research. Some professionals make the annual trek to Ocean City to find out about new tools and techniques and upcoming shows, and to see what other carvers are up to.

If you compete at the World and win, you'll heighten your visibility and enhance your name recognition. Top prizes can serve as stepping-stones to other income streams. Once you're perceived as a talented, award-winning carver, you may be asked to teach classes, write books, judge competitions, and participate in other income-producing activities. These activities, in turn, enhance your credibility and help build your collector base.

"When you compete, you stretch, and it's a real good growing experience," says Bill Veasey. "You need to take your lumps and grow. If you win a best of show at a little show, then go to Ocean City, where you may not even get an honorable mention. If you're going to compete, then really compete. Don't just pursue blue ribbons by doing off-beat birds in a show where there's a lot of competition among the more popular species, but where your bird will be the only one in its category. You may be apprehensive about moving up, because when you move up, the competition gets tougher. But you should always compete at your own level. Don't just stay at the same level until you've won one hundred ribbons. You're only kidding yourself."

If you decide to compete, keep in mind that the judging process isn't flawless. From time to time, competitions change their judging rules and procedures in an effort to improve fairness and objectivity, but the process still has its drawbacks.

"You have to have the desire to win," says Tan Brunet. "You need a lot of talent. You can't make a champion out of anyone. You have to watch out and not follow too much in other people's shadows. You have to stay original. You can't fool yourself. If you think another guy's better than you are, then you need to learn from him. And you have to be willing to take your beatings. I competed twice, in 1975 and 1976, before I won the World Championship."

"You need to have persistence," says Pat Godin. "Be there every year, and obviously try to improve the quality of your work. Challenge yourself. Every time you do something, do something different, a little unique.

"Some people think that if they could just win a World Championship, they'd be famous enough to make a lot of money. But whether you're trying to build your name through competition or exhibits, you have to keep your face and your work out there over the long term. You have to be there consistently from year to year. It's a long-term thing to market your work and to make your name recognizable. If you're there for the short term and drop out, people just don't remember you."

EVALUATING COST-EFFECTIVENESS

As you plan your show and competition schedule, realistically assess how long it will take and what it will cost to participate in each event. Bear in mind that the time spent traveling to, attending, and returning from a show is time away from your business. Packing and unpacking will also cut into your carving time. Also consider booth fees and whether show management requires a percentage of sales or requests additional donations (in dollars or artwork). Calculate the costs of shipping your artwork, the booth, promotional materials, and so on. You'll also need to pay for lodging (count the nights that you'll be on the road to and from the show), food, parking, and other miscellaneous expenses. If you'll be flying rather than driving, factor in the cost of your ticket. You should also consider what's known as an opportunity cost—your lack of productivity while you're away, and the sales you'll forgo if you have to close a retail outlet, particularly during tourist season.

"Some shows ask so much for a commission or percentage of sales that I won't do those shows," says Bob Guge. "Not all shows take percentages, but some do. They take care of your sales and say they'll send you a check in thirty days. That way they get their cut, and you're not going to cheat them. But you won't be able to use any money that you make in the show to pay for your trip. And some places even require a donation on top of all that. They're making all the money, and it's the poor artists who are supporting the causes. Then you've got to spend all the time to be there, and it costs so much for your hotel and other expenses. You have to sell so much just to break even before you can begin to make a profit."

JURIED SHOWS

The advantage of participation in juried shows may be prestige more than anything. Now you'll be able to list the exhibition among your credits. Your presence in shows of this sort will also help to create or maintain your image as a high-quality artist.

"Birds in Art is the most important show in bird art today anywhere," says Larry Barth. "Wausau has been heads above any other show anywhere artistically, and as far as class is involved. And it's gotten better every year. I think it's the most significant bird art event there is, just an incredibly exciting phenomenon. If you get a piece in that show, it's just wonderful. But in order to realize the full significance of having a piece in that show, you have to attend the event, and they get a very high percentage of attending artists for the opening. All you have to do is get to town, and they take care of you from there. There's a nonstop schedule of luncheons and receptions and dinners and private previews. They just take care of you; they make you feel like artists are the most important element of society. They treat you like royalty. And nowhere else does that happen.

"The most significant part of Wausau for me, and I think for a lot of artists, may not be the opening itself and the work that you see at the show, but the excitement and enthusiasm that you take home with you. I have a wonderful time at that opening, seeing that work and talking to those other artists. But as I drive home and then find myself back, by myself, in my studio, there's a heightened sense of awareness and a commitment to try to do the best that I can and do as much as I can. To me, that has probably been the most valuable part of Wausau—the excitement and the enthusiasm it instills in me and in the work I'm trying to do.

"I find it extremely beneficial to get together with like-minded individuals and compare notes and then go back to my own studio for another year of work. As an artist, I find myself working in isolation a good bit of the time. I'm here in my studio, with no coworkers and not all that much feedback. The Wausau show has become the highlight of my year."

THE ANATOMY OF A SUCCESSFUL SHOW
Create a High-Impact Display
Have you ever found yourself sitting in your exhibit booth at a selling show such as Easton, wondering why it seems that everyone just breezes by, barely even noticing you? Have some showgoers leaned over your work to look at the pieces on the table next to yours? The next time you're sitting at your table, watching carvers to your left and right make sales while you wonder why you're not, here are some questions to ask yourself about your display.

How is the table arranged? Does it include a variety of carvings or only one type? Are they of popular species? Diverse species? Are they painted in dull or brilliant colors? Is the work lined up in one row, all on one level? Or do you create tiers by stacking cubes, crates, or other elements? Are the carvings arranged in a pleasing, eye-catching, dynamic design that leads the viewers' gaze across the table? Note that there's a distinction between dynamic design and a busy display; you want the viewer to focus on your work.

Check out the displays of those who are successfully selling. Do they have lights? What kind? What kind of backdrops do they use? Do they use pedestals? Do they display carvings and sculptures on their table with no adornment whatsoever, or do they include decorative items? Are the tables covered? With what kind of material? Are their booths designed to draw visitors in, closer to the artwork and to the carver, who can then initiate a personal connection? What works?

"You want your storefront, your showroom window, to be the best in the show, so you need to dress it up," says Dan Williams. You can create an aesthetic display with different shapes, textures, and colorful materials. Rather than using neutral burlap to cover your table, try deep burgundy or royal blue velour. Drape it over the tops of boxes or crates to raise your pieces to different heights and bring them within the viewers' line of vision. Feature a diverse sampling of your work. Include some of your most recent carvings, as well as your best pieces. If possible, borrow pieces that you're proud of from collectors or customers, so that by viewing a quality assortment, potential buyers are exposed to a full spectrum of your skills.

If you've written books or been featured in a book, display them along the front edge of your table, clearly visible and readily accessible so that visitors can page through them. Have copies available for sale. If articles have been written about you, frame those that you're proud of and display them in the front or along the side walls of your booth. Highlight whatever you can to enhance your credibility and image.

Keep business cards, flyers, and brochures on hand so that those who visit your booth can take something with them. Even a business card will remind them of your carvings and make it easy to contact you later. Make it as easy as possible for someone to place an order.

Also take the opportunity to build a mailing list of prospects for future promotional efforts. Collect visitors' business cards in a fishbowl, or place a classy notebook on the table to encourage visitors to sign their names and addresses. You can sort these by zip code and notify prospects before your next exhibit or participation in a show in their locale.

Storytelling

When Bob Booth displays his carvings, he's promoting more than just a wooden bird—he's selling stories, folk art, and a little bit of history. Booth, a native of Chincoteague, Virginia, highlights his regional heritage in the design of his exhibit, which has repeatedly been selected by the Ward Foundation as the best booth display in the World Championship Wildfowl Carving Competition.

Booth says that he and his wife, Pixie, designed their display to resemble a house on Chincoteague Island. Blue and white wallpaper, cinched maroon floral curtains, and checkered burgundy fabric on the table contribute to the booth's homey atmosphere. Decoys, shorebirds, and silhouettes line a shelf high along the wall. And shorebird decoys hang from the shelf, strung together "as Chincoteague natives would have strung them to hang from their belts as they walked to and from the marsh to hunt," says Pixie. "When they reached the marshy area, they'd set them out, hunt over them, then string them back up so they could carry back what they'd shot."

Beneath the shelf along the top of the booth hangs a picture of the oyster-shucking house that Booth's father managed in the early 1900s. Another picture features Bob and his mother and father (who's carving), seated around the kitchen table in the family's apartment above the oyster-shucking house. Next to the picture, a painted scene of the marsh and geese is visible through one windowpane, and through another, you can see horses grazing along the water's edge.

In a pink cloth hat decorated with flowers, Pixie cheerfully greets showgoers while Bob, wearing red suspenders and a weathered captain's hat, carves decoys, strings birds, and tells stories. When anyone expresses even mild interest in a carving on his table or on the shelf, he provides a little background on the piece: "It's a little female ruddy, made to look like a decoy. It shows a little bit of wear, like a decoy would after it's been used." Throughout most of the shows that he and Pixie attend, Booth entertains visitors with Chincoteague memories and tales about his family, who helped settle the island in the 1700s:

"My daddy had to quit school in 1904. There were nine children in the family. He went to work with his daddy. At the age of nine, he was carrying an eight-gauge muzzle loader plus a shot bag and powder horn. As the tide rose in the marsh, they would shoot shorebirds or ducks and geese. As the tide went out, they'd be down in the mud flats catching clams and oysters.

"These look like the decoys that they'd use to hunt shorebirds. There was an abundance at market. Shorebirds were greatly sought by restaurants within a day's freight. Yellowlegs, plovers, curlews, and sandpipers were iced down in barrels and then served on the table in big restaurants. They would sell these. Pop would get anywhere from 12 to 15 cents a dozen for yellowlegs. My daddy would shoot at the thickest part when they'd jump to fly away. He would kill as many as forty-five yellowlegs at a shooting."

Interpersonal Skills

Many carvers overlook one of the most important aspects of a successful show: the need to be physically present in your booth all or most of the time that the show's in progress. "The quality of your work is of permanent importance, but you have to be at the show to sell yourself as well," says Pat Godin. "Think of it as an overall strategy. At a show like Easton, you're going to make more contacts with buyers if you're standing at your table. At competitions, the worst thing you can do is to take your birds there Friday night and then pick them up at the end of the weekend."

Some collectors prefer purchasing their artwork at shows, directly from the carvers, rather than going to a gallery. Along with avoiding the gallery's commission, the collector gets to meet the artist. "I'm convinced that for most collectors, a major part of the fun of collecting is getting to know the carvers, conversing with them, coming to the shows and talking to them," says Pat Godin. "If you're not there, they can't get to know you. A lot of collectors don't want to deal with someone else."

Although shows such as the Easton Waterfowl Festival have "booth sitters," and you might be able to lasso a family member or friend to watch your booth for a while, some potential customers will buy only when the artist is actually present. You're also more likely to close a sale if you're there in person to knowledgeably answer questions and discuss your work. Visitors are often responsive to personable carvers who are in their booths and eager to meet people. Part of selling your artwork is selling your personality. When something that you've carved decorates someone's home, your piece may have more meaning if the customer can picture you.

More important than what's on your table is to pay attention to the people, Dan Williams believes. "When people come to an exhibit and are contemplating buying art, the piece that they're looking at and thinking about buying is actually a small part of the sale," he says. "The bigger part of the sale is that people want to know you as the artist. You've got basically two or three minutes to make a connection with these people, and if you don't make the connection within that time, kiss them good-bye. They're gone. But if you can make that connection, then they'll stay there, they'll talk to you, they'll feel comfortable with you, they'll get to know you and feel that you're trustworthy—whatever you can convey to them—and they may then buy the piece. And this is true with anything that you're going to sell.

"To make that connection, you have to be right up front with them. You can't be sitting behind your table reading a magazine, drinking a beer, or chitchatting with the guy at the table behind you, totally ignoring the crowd. I see this all the time at shows, and then those are the same guys who are always complaining that it was a terrible show, terrible show, they didn't sell a thing. And I walk out of there with ten or fifteen grand in my pocket because I don't do that. I make it a point of always being around my table. I don't go walking around, chitchatting with the boys all weekend. It's a business. That's my storefront and I treat it as such. I stay there, I talk to people, I'm friendly. I try to make eye contact with people. I sell."

Ernie Muehlmatt, on the other hand, says, "I don't hang around my table too much. I make people think that I must not really need this sale. I must be doing really well. It's a head game. They think that because I don't seem to care, they should buy my work. I think people like to be left alone, and if they want it, they'll find you. You don't impulse buy $5,000 pieces. You think about it."

The next time you're at a show, watch some of the top-name professionals and note their personal styles. Whether solo or with their families, most have personalities that distinguish them from the crowd. And their interpersonal skills are an asset when they deal with collectors. Whether laughing over drinks during cocktail hour or discussing details regarding their next commission, the pros seem to devote their undivided attention to collectors' concerns.

Social skills offer a definite advantage, not only at shows, but in business in general. If you're shy, you need to find ways to force yourself to be more outgoing. "I was shy, and I still am sort of shy, but certainly in a show situation or most any professional situation, I've learned to talk to people," says Bart Walter. "It's made a big difference. If you can make a personal connection with people, it certainly is important for repeat buyers, and I think it's important at shows in general. It's not always easy to do if you're a shy person."

NETWORKING

Networking is one of the most effective tools you can use to enhance your exposure and gain recognition. Volunteer within your community, and get involved in activities that address issues that concern you. If you share common ground with other participants, your focus on mutual interests may minimize self-consciousness and help you become more comfortable in social settings.

New personal and professional connections will broaden your potential customer base. "Once you feel that you've got good carving skills, then it's time to start talking to friends, to relatives, to start networking broader and broader, farther and farther afield," says Bart Walter. "Frequently, in woodcarving particularly, you'll find some people who are interested in purchasing your work.

"I've stayed in contact with a lot of interesting people that I've met over the course of my life. I'm very into what I do, very serious, very committed, and people pick up on that. And if they're at all interested in what I do, and I'm interested in what they do, I try to keep in touch, or at least know what they're up to. Maintaining contact helps get your name out there. These people know of your work, and if they have a photograph, or a catalog, or something of yours, and the subject of bird carving comes up, they can say, 'Oh yes, I know somebody, I've got a photograph.' It makes a big difference. It's better advertising than going to an art show."

Get involved with raptor centers, art associations, maybe even your local historical society. Although you won't be making money when you're not carving, consider making connections as an investment. One of the best organizations for carvers and artists to get involved with is Ducks Unlimited, Inc. There are over thirty-five hundred DU chapters throughout the country, and each chapter holds an auction banquet at least once a year. Carvers sometimes donate their work outright or make arrangements with the local DU chapter to receive a percentage of their auction profits.

Donations of your work will help DU raise funds and you'll sometimes get unexpected mileage out of your contribution. You'll heighten your profile as a local carver, and frequently your exposure will lead to additional sales. Occasionally the donation of a larger-than-usual carving has attracted the attention of wealthy executives at DU events and led to subsequent high-end commissions for some carvers.

"I developed methods of marketing some of my carvings through some of these auctions," says Bill Veasey. "Most people put a very insignificant, cheap item in these auctions. That's the wrong strategy. We're dealing with a very sophisticated buying public today. And so in their sophistication, they're not going to pay very much for something that isn't very well done, that isn't a good carving. So consequently, if you're going to participate in something like this, you're better off putting a good piece in there and generating a good buck for it. It doesn't have to be your best work, but it should be good work. For instance, a lot of artists will put in a shrink-wrapped print in which they have a total cost of $2, and they expect to get some money for it. Well, if they would stick a $40 or $50 or $60 frame on the thing, they could probably get a couple hundred bucks. It's like the old cliché, penny-wise and pound-foolish. But if you put in a better piece, DU will get more money, you may get more money, and you'll get more notice."

Your involvement with DU will also introduce you to professionals in your community, which can open up other promotional avenues. You may be able to barter with physicians, dentists, and others you meet at local fund-raising events. "You can trade your carvings for eyeglasses, dental work, and other work," says Georgia Dayhoff. "If doctors and dentists are willing to put your carvings in their offices, where they will be seen by the public, you can get a lot of commissions that way." When you work out this sort of arrangement, place a stock of business cards and promotional literature alongside the pieces on display.

Try to establish yourself as a local authority on the subject of bird carving or its history. Consider offering a one-time lecture or teaching a noncredit course called Introduction to Bird Carving in evening classes at the local high school or community college. Find out if there's a local speakers' bureau where you live or whether the local nature center is interested in speakers, and ask them to contact you if a community group is interested in a presentation on the history of bird carving or on a particular species with which you're familiar. If people who attended your presentation subsequently recognize your work in a gift shop, they'll likely take notice.

DEALING WITH THE MEDIA

"I've always gone out of my way to get press for my work," says Pat Godin. "If somebody wants to interview me, nothing is too trivial. I always accommodate them. Always go out of your way to get any press that you can for your work. Press coverage is pretty significant, even something local. You never know what's going to come out of it or who will see it."

If your work starts appearing in juried art shows and winning top prizes in competitions, the events' publicity specialists may feature you in some of their promotional materials. You might be mentioned in news releases sent to print and broadcast media, including national magazines. You'll benefit by getting some national exposure without having to bear the news release printing and mailing costs. To maximize your local exposure regarding these events, ask the publicists to include your local media in their mailings. Provide them with labels or a list of your local media contacts. Though exposure in national magazines will enhance your image and might lead to commissions, an announcement or story about you in your local newspaper is more likely to generate phone calls and more immediate response.

Unless you've hired a public relations specialist, you'll need to pursue your own publicity. Local newspapers are often looking for free copy, and if it's well written or even just a little better than average, they may accept it. If you have writing skills, consider contributing a weekly or occasional column to the paper. Your involvement with DU may help you persuade the editor to accept a column on birding, hunting, or environmental topics. Again, think in terms of positioning yourself as a local expert on subjects related to your carving. If you find writing difficult or you can't afford to take time away from your carving, consider hiring a freelancer or reporter to ghostwrite a column for you. If you see the designation "correspondent" after someone's name in the local paper, you might be able to interest him or her in a freelance writing assignment. When someone ghosts for you, you'll still get the byline and the exposure, but you'll be able to devote more time to your carving.

Start a file of newspaper or magazine clips. Include articles about you and any columns you may have written. If the articles are well written and would serve as good promotional pieces, save multiple copies, request reprints, or pay for some high-quality color copies to distribute to select targets. You can also frame the original articles and post them in your exhibit booth.

News Releases

News releases are one of the easiest and least expensive ways to get the word out about you and your work. The goal of the news release is to alert the media to something about yourself and your carving and, depending on the topic, to motivate the editor to either print the release verbatim or send someone out to write a feature story about you. The better the news release, in terms of the quality of writing and the information that you submit, and the less need for editing, the more likely that the newspaper will pick up your text verbatim. The likelihood of your release being printed will also be influenced by how well you've targeted your message to your audience—in this case, both the editor and readers. You have to first get the attention of the editor and demonstrate that your topic will be of interest to readers. You'll have a better chance of accomplishing this if you familiarize yourself with the publication and make sure that the topic of your release is relevant to its readers.

Editors receive hundreds of releases each week, so there has to be something extraordinary, exciting, or unique in your announcement to make it stand out. Try to focus your release on a "news peg"—timely, interesting, and newsworthy information that will make the editor want to run your story *today*. Releases with news pegs are likely to be run sooner than "evergreens," topics that will retain their interest or vitality for a while. If you've just won a ribbon at a local, regional, or national show, send a news release to your local media as soon as possible. Don't delay your mailing for weeks or even days. Lack of timeliness is one of the primary reasons editors toss releases into the trash.

Once you understand the basic formula, news releases are fairly simple to write. Just keep your target audience in mind as you make decisions about what to include and what not to. The key to writing a successful release is to have a clear, focused message and to make your topic relevant to readers' lives. What can you say in the first paragraph that will grab the readers' attention? What aspect of your announcement has the most human interest? How is your carving relevant to the readers' world?

To get started, list the five essential five Ws, the conventional formula for newspaper leads: *who*, *what*, *where*, *when*, and *why*. If relevant, you can also tack on *how*. Once you've listed these elements, writing the release is simply a matter of stringing them together in cohesive paragraph form. But before you worry about the arrangement of paragraphs, add a sentence or two to provide a little more detail about each W. You should now have an expanded list.

These elements have traditionally been included close to the beginning of a newspaper story. If you follow this tradition and your release is well written, you'll create an attention-getting lead, or introduction, and the editor won't have to dig to find out what you're talking about. You might then include some additional information, such as a little art-related biographical detail about yourself, details on your work, the award that you've won, the organization that hosted the event you're describing, or other relevant background.

Your release should be informative but not wordy. Although you need to be concise, make sure that you include the five Ws and other important details. Failure to include critical elements may result in holes in your release. Missing pieces of information or failure to anticipate readers' questions could cause an editor not to run your announcement.

Your text should be clear, concise, and credible. Make sure the details in your release are accurate and spelled correctly. Pay particular attention to names, dates, places, and addresses. Your release should be written in terms that the average reader will understand, so avoid jargon and technical terms, such as the names of high-tech tools.

The topic of the release should dictate whether you mail it to national or local newspapers and magazines, or both. Before mailing to magazines, find out the name and title of the specific editor who handles news about carving and other facets of wildlife art. On the local level, direct your releases to the newspaper's features editor or whoever is responsible for coverage of the arts. Specific editors handle various departments within a newspaper or magazine, and by directing your release to the appropriate editor, you're more likely to get the coverage you're seeking. Increasingly, news releases are being distributed on-line or via fax, so check with the editor you'll be dealing with most frequently to find out which method of delivery he or she prefers.

In addition to submitting news releases to the media, some carvers occasionally call their local editors to pitch a feature story idea. This tactic can be most effective when you have an unusual news peg, but use it sparingly. Editors are busy people and may not be receptive if you're always badgering them for publicity. Before you try this approach, find out when your local paper goes to press, and avoid calling the editor in the hectic hours before a deadline. You might also call radio and television news directors if your news peg will be conducive to broadcast coverage and sound bites (for example, the opening of your one-person show).

When you submit photographs with your news release, clearly identify each photo with the name, address, and phone number of the supplier or the person who holds the copyright. Print this information on the reverse of the photo; use a felt-tip pen or a stamp to protect the image. If a museum or another organization provides the photo, include a courtesy credit line ("Photo courtesy of . . ."). Instead of using glue or paper clips, use rubber cement to attach captions to photos, and check the accuracy of names, dates, and other details included in the caption.

Print your release on "news release" letterhead, which you can design yourself with desktop publishing software. Provide the name, address, and phone and fax numbers of a contact person in case the editor or reporter has any questions about the information in your release.

Limit your release to one or two pages, if possible, three pages maximum. If you run on to a second page, type "MORE" in the center of the bottom of the first page, and "###" or "-30-" at the end of the release. At the top of page two, type your name, the release title, and "Add One" (which in newspaper terms indicates that it's page two). There are minor variations in news release formats. The following sample (on page 73) provides a basic format that you can follow to give your release a professional look.

Reasons to Generate a News Release

This is by no means a comprehensive listing, but it should give you an idea of when to generate a news release and how to create a news peg.

- You've just established your business and want to announce it to the community.
- You'll be displaying your work at a one-person show in the local bank, library, museum, art institute, nature center, or historical society. Check with the person hosting the show to see if he or she will be promoting the event. If so, you might want to coordinate your efforts.
- You recently won a carving competition at the local, regional, or national level. Even placing first as a novice or intermediate can help get you recognized and heighten your profile as a local artist.
- You've created a carving in response to a widely publicized environmental issue or event, such as Earth Day, an oil spill, or the identification of a newly endangered species. Editors often look for ways to give local slants to global issues.

NEWS FROM
THE QUITTAPAHILLA WILDLIFE CARVING STUDIO

Contact: Joan Smith
Creek Drive, Annville, PA 17003
Phone/Fax: 717-777-7777
E-mail: jmsmith@xxx.xxx
http: www.xxxxxxxxxxxx

FOR IMMEDIATE RELEASE

SMITH PLACES FIRST AT THE 19XX WARD FOUNDATION WORLD CHAMPIONSHIP WILDFOWL CARVING COMPETITION

Annville, PA, (Date)—Joan Smith, a professional wildlife carver and native of Annville, Pa., recently won first prize in the Decorative Lifesize Division at the 19XX Ward World Championship Wildfowl Carving Competition in Ocean City, Md. This year, more than XX,XXX carvers from around the world competed in the annual World Championship, the largest event of its kind. Since 1971, the show has recognized outstanding carvers for their contribution to the original American art form of decoy carving.

Smith was awarded first prize for her life-size carving of a chickadee, one of numerous songbird species that frequent the feeders that surround her studio. Situated along the banks of central Pennsylvania's Quittapahilla Creek, Smith's studio provides an unobstructed view of the creek and the Quittie Nature Park. The park, a preserved natural area, provides an ideal habitat for various avian subjects such as doves and cardinals, which are featured in her carvings. The view from her studio provides an opportunity for Smith and her carving students to observe and carve these species while they're undisturbed in their natural environment. Smith offers classes in her studio year-round.

Smith, a professional carver since 1979, has won numerous prizes and has been featured in major juried art shows such as XXXXX throughout the country.

To see her carvings or sign up for classes, stop by the Quittapahilla Wildlife Carving Studio, Creek Drive, Annville, Pa., 17003 from 9 a.m. to 5 p.m. on Mon., Wed., Fri., and Sat., or call 717-777-7777 to set up an appointment at your convenience. To learn more about the artist, carving, and classes, stop by her studio or check out her home page at http:xxxxxx.

###

- You'll be hosting an open house in your studio, workshop, or home. (Also try to get events of this type listed in local calendars of events, and post notices on billboards and in other venues around your community. Pay attention to calendar deadlines, which are sometimes months in advance of the events.)
- You're opening a carving school or will be offering classes in your studio.
- You'll be branching out into another line of carving, a different kind of waterfowl, or another wildlife species.
- You've expanded your repertoire, will be working in new mediums, or offering a new instructional product line.

SHOULD YOU ADVERTISE?

Although a lot of carvers have fared well without advertising, don't rule it out. Its utility will depend on the profile of your business. It may not be cost-effective to advertise your one-of-a-kind, original woodcarvings, but if you're teaching classes or producing limited editions in bronze, it could be a productive way to get the word out. Along with targeting ads to art collectors, browse newsstands to discover other magazines targeted to readers interested in the subjects you carve.

Even if you've decided not to advertise your one-of-a-kind carvings, consider at least occasionally buying ad space to promote your classes, a line of instructional videotapes, or other facets of your business. Investigate the possibility of advertising in specialized supplements that sometimes piggyback local newspapers when shows are in progress, such as the supplement in the *Star Democrat*, Easton's newspaper. Think about running ads on a local or national level in conjunction with a show. For example, if you'll be displaying your work at the local high school or running a carving class in your area, buy some space in the local newspaper and run a high-quality photograph along with a caption that reads, "You'll see (your name)'s work at (date, time, place)." Or if you're creating limited editions of your work in bronze, consider advertising in an issue of *Wildlife Art* that will be published around the time of a major annual wildlife art exhibition that will attract collectors from all over the country.

Although an advertisement may not result in an immediate sale, your presence among the pages of a slick magazine is apt to enhance your image, and if someone who saw the ad spots your work in a gallery, that recognition may be the critical factor in making a sale. After you establish an ongoing relationship with a gallery, its owner or director may purchase advertising space to display your work or ask you to split the cost of a cooperative advertisement.

TRACKING PROMOTIONAL EFFECTIVENESS

It's often tough to track promotional effectiveness, and a sale that may seem to be the result of a casual referral may sometimes be attributable to another form of promotion. For example, if someone phones you or wanders into your studio upon the recommendation of a friend, you may not realize that the customer tracked you down because he or she had spotted the blue ribbon beside your work at the recent World Championship or had learned from a friend that you had placed there. Or he or she may have recalled a feature story about your involvement in the local chapter of DU that had run in the local paper months before.

It can also take a while to reap the benefits of specific promotional efforts, the results of which are not always readily or precisely quantifiable. Take a given show, for example. You dressed well, had an attention-getting display, saw a fair amount of traffic in your booth, and interacted with as many potential customers as possible. Nevertheless, the show was a disappointment, and you went home with less-than-optimal cash sales. But then, three months later and seemingly out of nowhere, someone who was impressed by your work at the show but didn't have the money at the time calls and places a large order.

Although it's difficult to track promotional effectiveness, it's worthwhile to try to evaluate the cost-effectiveness of various methods you've employed. Keep track of your promotional expenses and, as much as possible, monitor response. Your promotional plan should be based upon your current understanding of your market, but as you implement your preliminary plan, you'll get feedback on what works and what doesn't. This sort of feedback can provide valuable marketing research information and other data that can help you as you plan future strategies to reach your target markets.

CHAPTER 6

The Business of Carving

GETTING STARTED

Every business, even one that's home-based, needs a plan to ensure success. Although you may get lucky in your first foray into the business of carving, haphazard financing and poor management practices could spell disaster. A plan will help improve your chances for success. It need not be engraved in stone; you can modify it as necessary.

The business planning process should include an idea of where you want to be professionally and personally for at least the next five years. If you've done your marketing homework, you should have identified your products and have a pretty good idea of the *who* and *where* of your target markets. In addition to specifying your marketing mix, your business plan should integrate budgeting, tax considerations, health and life insurance planning, and even retirement. As you gain experience, these considerations will seem less overwhelming, but in the meantime, you might seek advice from business, finance, law, and insurance professionals. These experts can help you establish realistic estimates of income and expenses and prepare financial analyses such as a cash flow statement, profit and loss statement, and balance sheet.

Interpersonal skills will be an asset as you deal with professionals, suppliers, collectors, gallery directors, gift shop owners, and others. If you're not comfortable dealing with the public, look for a college or evening school course in public speaking or customer relations. You can develop other business-related skills by participating in workshops and seminars conducted by the Small Business Administration or the local chamber of commerce.

You need to be well organized and manage your time wisely. You have to realistically evaluate and anticipate deadlines, prioritize tasks, and schedule production accordingly. At least a simple inventory system is necessary to track the coming and going of raw materials and finished carvings. This tracking needs to be done for accounting and tax purposes, and it will help ensure that you don't run out of a specific type of wood or paint when you're up against a deadline. If you're not organized, you'll undoubtedly run into scheduling conflicts, miss show application deadlines, and possibly gain a reputation for failing to deliver your wholesale orders or commissioned artwork on time.

SETTING UP YOUR WORKSPACE

Some businesses begin with less than $1,000 in start-up funds. And if you've been carving as a hobby for a while, you may own most of the tools you'll need to start a business. Established carvers' opinions vary as to what's needed to succeed as a professional. Some feel that you're at a significant disadvantage unless you invest a lot of money in high-tech, high-speed tools to keep your work up to par with current competitive standards; others say that you can get started with a relatively small investment.

"You can carve birds without spending a whole lot of money," says Bob Guge. "You could get started with a couple hundred bucks—with a Dremel tool, a small woodburner, a few bits, and a few odds and ends. You could probably do that for $200. When you add a Foredom for doing big work, that's about another $200. I would say that for $500, you could carve anything you wanted. You can get by without a band saw when you're starting out. There are a lot of ways to obtain cutouts. You can go to lumberyards, or you can have friends cut things out for you. You really don't need many things. I won the World Championship two times when all I had was a Dremel tool and a woodburner. The sophisticated tools aren't necessities."

Your start-up costs will depend on your current skills, professional objectives, how aggressively you plan to compete, and the equipment you already have. For more advice, talk to full-time carvers, consult reference books and magazines dealing with techniques, and explore some of the woodcarving resources on the Internet (see chapter 3).

You may already have a workspace or workshop set up in your home or garage. If you're thinking about building such an area, which will then become part of your home office (for tax purposes), budget carefully. A basic tenet in the establishment of a home business is to contain costs. Have more than one builder take a look at the space that you'd like to dedicate to your business, and tell them that you're trying to contain costs. Ask the builders for hints on how to maximize the usable space for the greatest efficiency and productivity, and then compare their estimates. Until you're established, function should be most important; you can probably postpone the expense of carpeting, window coverings, and other decorative elements.

SETTING UP YOUR OFFICE

Once you have a workspace or workshop, have all the necessary tools, and have been carving for a while, you might need additional space to conduct your business. It can be frustrating to try to find and organize statements, inquiries, invoices, and receipts if they're buried under tools, paint supplies, sketches, and carvings in progress. You should establish and preserve a specific location as your business office. Try to set aside a separate room or a section of your workshop for this purpose, and not part of your living space. You may have to show an IRS representative your home office if your tax deduction is questioned.

Just as your shop or studio is set up to give you the most productive creative environment, your office should be designed to help organize sales, communications, and record keeping. You shouldn't need a lot of space, but you will need enough room for a desk and comfortable chair, computer system, filing system, bookshelves, and maybe some display shelves. Since zoning laws are not uniform from community to community and may vary within a specific community, be sure to check with city or county officials to learn whether there are any restrictions on home businesses where you live.

A computer is almost essential to run a profitable business. Among other tasks, you can use the computer to track inventory, keep books, do taxes, generate bills, conduct financial analyses, create a variety of promotional communications, and maintain a customer database and a schedule of shows.

As a general rule, as long as you purchase a quality computer, it can be upgraded to meet future needs. Discuss your needs with a qualified computer consultant (not an apathetic clerk at the local discount electronics store), and find a computer that has a high-speed processor, large hard drive, fast modem with a graphical user interface, excellent graphics capabilities, an oversize monitor, and a CD-ROM. Whatever your personal bias with regard to operating systems, most quality computers come bundled with software that will give you access to the Internet, E-mail capability, word processing, spreadsheets, databases, and graphics. You may need to purchase software beyond these basics, depending on your personal requirements.

Spreadsheet programs such as Microsoft Excel or Lotus 1-2-3 will facilitate setting up your accounting system. Even if you plan to hire an accountant to help do your books or taxes, a good spreadsheet program can simplify your day-to-day recording of cash receipts and disbursements. You might also explore accounting software that will help you set up your bookkeeping system, maintain a general ledger, and keep track of income and expenses.

Desktop-publishing software can be used to generate attention-getting brochures and newsletters. If your budget allows, get a color laser printer to go with your computer system; there's no substitute for the quality graphic output of a laser printer. A high-quality scanner is also useful because it will allow you to import text and photographic images of your work into the computer. Images can then be "pasted" into brochures for mailing, or they can be placed on a home page that you might develop as your personal Web site. Your computer and a digital camera can be used to generate photographic images of your work, which can then be transmitted via E-mail to collectors, gallery directors, and other target markets.

It may take some time to become familiar with your word-processing, spreadsheet, desktop-publishing and other programs, but in the long run, it will be a worthwhile investment. Make sure that you don't get lost surfing the Net, though, or let your computer become a time-waster rather than time-saver. "I've seen some people get really locked into the computer world, trying to figure out all the different ways they can use it," says Leo Osborne. "They're so locked into the computer that they spend two years doing that and don't create anything. I've seen that really become a problem with people, where the business can overrun the artistic creativity."

As you set up your office, you'll need a fax machine, business phone, and answering machine or voice mail system. You'll also need to stock up on stationery including business cards, all-purpose letterhead, and news release letterhead. If you plan to take your own pictures, you'll need equipment for taking and storing photographs, including a 35mm and possibly a digital camera, film, slide viewer or light table, slide folders, and binders. Keep all these items in mind as you're calculating expenses.

Your telephone is your link to collectors, suppliers, gallery owners, and all other prospects. Consider getting a separate phone line for your business. The business line will be fully tax-deductible, as will any business-related long-distance charges, optional services such as voice mail or call waiting, and related equipment such as fax machines and modems. Depending on your product line and whether you have a studio showroom, you might also want to have a yellow pages listing. Although it will be an additional expense, the listing will help potential customers find your business.

An answering machine or voice mail system, available through your phone company, is a necessity in today's business world. Your message should be concise and professional, and there should be sufficient space on your tape for callers to complete their response. For callers' convenience, you might want to include your fax number as part of your phone message. So as not to miss a potential lead, if you have two phone lines, you might also consider subscribing to voice mail combined with a rollover option that switches a call to your second line if your primary business line is busy.

LEARNING TO BUDGET

It's wise to contain costs right from the start. Be prudent in your initial outlays for carving supplies and other variable expenses (costs of production). Once you have an accurate idea of your fixed expenses (costs of operating the business), you'll be in a better position to determine how much you can allocate to promotion and to other expenses that can be increased and decreased from month to month.

Although they're subject to some fluctuation, fixed expenses are recurrent items that can't easily be changed. One of your fixed costs, for example, will be based on the percentage of space that your workshop and office occupy within your home. This will determine the percentage of your rent or mortgage that you can allocate as a business operating expense.

At the start, you'll be relying on *estimates* of income and expenses, so it's essential that you learn to budget carefully. When the cash comes in from the sale of your first few carvings, realize that you're likely to encounter some dry spells and set aside some reserves. After you've been in business awhile, you'll have an idea of your cash flow—the amount of cash that you'll have available at various points in time. Learn how to calculate and regularly monitor cash flow, particularly if you intend to create intricate, one-of-a-kind carvings. Although you may anticipate a profit following the completion of a major piece, you could go broke in the meantime if you haven't wisely managed your money.

"You can go to a show and take in $5,000, but the next two shows may be a blank," says Bill Veasey. "If you want to make a living at this, you have to manage your money so that there's a cash flow. Your kids have to eat every week. You have to know what your expenses are. You have to know what you have to produce. You have to break that down into weeks, days, and hours to determine production. You have to build up a cash reserve and not spend it. Regardless of how much inventory you have—let's say you have twenty pieces and you haven't sold anything—you still have to produce whatever you have to produce every day. It may not sell today, it may not sell tomorrow, but ultimately it will sell."

In the first year, your budget will fluctuate somewhat, and you'll need to regularly update and revise your actual and predicted income and expenses. Your computer will come in handy as you track unforeseen expenditures, and after a few months you should be able to predict overhead expenses with a reasonable degree of accuracy. Your overhead will include operating expenses like insurance, repairs and maintenance of equipment, and the relevant percentage of rent or mortgage and utility payments.

Perhaps you've already sold some of your work and feel pretty good about the price people were willing to pay for your creations. "People get into trouble because they don't realize how things change when they start carving full-time," says Phil Galatas. "You might sell a piece for $1,800, and when you're doing it part-time, that's fine if you're comfortable with that. But once you're in business, $1,800 might not be enough, because you also have to consider expenses. It take tools to get these things done. You have to turn on the lights, turn on the heat, and pay for health insurance, vehicles, rent or mortgage. Let's say your airbrush breaks and you have to pay to get it fixed. And you still haven't paid taxes. A lot of people just don't think about this."

When you're self-employed, the income from your carvings will also be used to pay for publications, show entry fees, and all the other expenses associated with shows. "To figure out your cost of sales, you need to consider every single thing you spend," says Bill Veasey. "Even for air conditioning. It isn't a luxury. It's really something that you need to consider. Your shop has to be comfortable, or you're not going to be productive. If you're hot, you won't be producing."

As your skills improve and you command more money for your work, you may find yourself working on one piece for months. Although you might anticipate $15,000 or more when the piece is finished, unless you've established other income streams or have arranged to receive installment payments as the work progresses, it may be tough to survive without supplemental income during those months.

"Budgeting is really important, and I haven't always been that great at it," says Floyd Scholz. "I used to have a problem when I'd get a big check. I'd think, man, I'm rich—let's party! That happened a few times. I bought a couple of nice things, and then suddenly, uh-oh, I was only halfway through the next bird and out of cash. What do you do? You have to be very careful about that. You have to discipline yourself and have a long-range perspective on where the money will be needed. That's the value of having some type of a financial plan."

Spouses or others often play an important role in the carving business. Says Bart Walter, "A key ingredient in being an artist with integrity and trying to do it professionally is to have someone to support you for the first couple years—someone who really likes your work and is willing to help you out, be it a relative, a spouse or a benefactor. It's very rare to start carving, or any art, and be able to pursue it full-time. In my case, it was my wife who supported me when I started full-time. I didn't earn diddly for the first couple years."

Unless you can partially rely on someone else's income as you get started or have the economic luxury to pursue your passion full-time, hang on to your day job, or at least get a part-time job until you're certain that there's a reliable—well, as reliable as it gets—demand for your work. On average, this could take anywhere from five to ten years if you follow the pattern of the pros. In the meantime, if you quit your full-time job to take a part-time position, you'll probably need to pick up your own health and life insurance and contribute to a retirement plan.

"Don't just dive into the deep end of the pool; wade into the shallow end first," says Floyd Scholz. "Until you get established and get a collector base established, you need to have a reliable means of income to pay your electric bill, your mortgage or rent, and your insurance. Unless you're sort of a Bohemian type who lives in a trailer and couldn't care less, you need to have some other means of income until you can guarantee that you've got enough commissions lined up to keep a cash flow coming in. When I started out, I worked in a lumberyard for about a year."

PRICING

Figuring out how to price your work will be one of your biggest challenges as a self-employed professional. If you're only carving one-of-a-kind items, your best pricing strategy may be largely intuitive. If you get into mass production or start casting in bronze, pricing formulas can be useful, but there is no clear-cut way to know which pricing strategy is right for you.

Some self-employed carvers use cost-oriented methods such as break-even pricing, which determines the level of sales needed to cover all of the relevant fixed and variable costs. But cost-oriented formulas don't always account for variations in demand or productivity. And if you're just starting out, you may not yet have enough experience to accurately assess your costs, productivity, and seasonal fluctuations.

After you've been carving for a while and have reliable financial data, you'll be able to base your pricing decisions on your competitors' prices, your own costs and margins, and ultimately, what your target markets are willing to pay for your work.

Most professionals recommend going-rate pricing, a strategy in which you set prices equal to, or a certain percentage above or below, competitors' prices. Whether this method is appropriate for you depends on several factors, including your costs, competitors' costs, how many carvings you're able to produce, and customers' perceptions of your carvings compared with others'.

"You need to get out there and see what you're competing against in the marketplace, and also to figure out what you need to earn," says Leo Osborne. "Very few people can start off with really high prices. It's a matter of getting out there and seeing your competition. If similar sculptures or carvings are priced at half of what you want to get, what makes yours worth twice the price? You really have to balance that out and look at your competition. It may be that a lot of detail has gone into your work, and maybe it's taken a lot more time, and sometimes people will spend more because of that."

"The hardest part in pricing is having to stand back and be objective about your own work," says Bill Veasey. "You have to be able to recognize whose work yours is on a level with, not just expect to get $5,000 a bird because one carver is asking that much for his work."

Bob Guge, who initially pursued carving on a part-time basis while working as a house painter, says that right from the start, he knew he eventually wanted to do it professionally. "I knew that to carve full-time, I'd have to make as much as I did in my regular job or it wouldn't work. So I took my hourly wage as a painter and figured how much I'd have to charge for a bird, depending on how many hours it took me to complete it. That's how I started out. Sometimes I made out well; sometimes I didn't. But it averaged out, and eventually, after I'd been carving full-time and realized that I didn't have any birds sitting on my shelf, I figured it was time to raise the price a little bit. And that's what I did every year. There have been a number of ups and downs, and in the times when birds weren't selling well, I didn't increase prices."

Pat Godin says that even though your most significant investment in an original carving will be the time that you spend on the piece, "in the beginning, you're not going to make very much an hour. When you're a beginning carver, you're going to have to pay your dues. As an entrepreneur selling bird carvings, you just hope that you'll be able to elevate the prices to the point that you feel you're making a reasonable amount. It's not realistic to think that you can just quit your job and start making a living and charging high prices right from scratch. You have to build a name for yourself. It's an unfortunate fact that initially you'll have to sell your work for less than what you think it's worth. Even today, I often feel this way."

You may be able to charge a little more for a carving if it has appeared in juried shows, had a lot of exposure at wildlife art exhibitions, or won an award in a competition, particularly the World Championship. "The enthusiasm that a gallery owner has for your work is also important," says Leo Osborne. "And sometimes people will spend more on a bigger piece." You can also balance the price against the complexity of the pose, advises Floyd Scholz. "For instance, if one of your red-tailed hawks has open wings, an open mouth, and a spread tail, it should be priced higher than one that's less dramatic, with wings that are just folded."

Find out what other carvers are getting for their work by visiting gift shops and attending bird-carving and wildlife art shows. "A good place to see other work is the Easton Waterfowl Festival, where all the birds have prices on them," says Floyd Scholz. "You can get a feel for what the market will bear for your level of work." You can also investigate what galleries are charging for comparable wood sculptures. However, there is so much variation in gallery markups that the retail price may provide little indication of what the gallery paid (or will pay) the carver for the piece. Whereas gift shops typically rely on a keystone markup—100 percent, or double the wholesale price—the pricing structure among galleries may be more reliant on the demographics of their specific market. For example, galleries in large cities or in high-end locations often have a higher markup.

"When you're trying to get established, set your prices at least one notch lower than what you see around you so that you can establish a value for your work," says Bart Walter. "You want to establish an increasing value for your work, gradually raising your price to where your peers are. Then you should be able to raise your prices even more, and keep going up and up. That way the collector feels like he's getting a good return on the money he's investing in your work. It's very important, but it's an often overlooked component."

"I look at what other people are putting out and what I can do for the same money," says Pati Stajcar. "I want to put out a quality piece, and I'm not trying to undercut my competition, but a lot of artists have other jobs, and I have to eat. I base my prices on the size of the piece and what the market will bear. My prices will be lower than those of many other carvers because I don't have the time to let my work sit on the shelf and wait for the dime when I can sell it now for the quick nickel."

Sometimes carvers price their work on the high side to convey an impression of quality. "A lot of people think that if a carving is not expensive, it's not any good," says Eldridge Arnold. "I think that's true in a lot of cases—the cheaper work is not very good. When you start pricing your work, if you price it too low, then customers will get the feeling that it's not any good." You have to be careful how you do it, but pricing for quality can be an effective strategy, as long as you're delivering a quality product and your price seems fair to customers.

If your prices are too high, this approach is likely to backfire. "Make sure that you don't get a false illusion of what your work is worth," says Jim Sprankle. "Carvers often go to a DU auction and sell their work for a high price because it's a donation write-off for the purchaser. This gives carvers the mistaken perception that their work is worth more than it is, and then they price themselves out of the market."

"Pricing is an area that's very difficult," says Dave Ahrendt. "Carvers tend to see one person sell a carving for a high price, say $2,000, and theirs looks kind of like it, so they decide to price their piece for $2,000. If they do sell it, this gives them the impression that they can sell every piece they do for $2,000, but that may not be the case. That one sale may have just been a lucky situation. If you're going to make a living at this, you can't base all your prices on one sale; you have to compare your work with other similar carvings in a market similar to yours."

Pat Godin says, "Once you start to establish a value for your work and have had some success in competitions, you might start increasing the price of your work. But it shouldn't be too great an increase. I still have to be careful about overpricing so that a piece doesn't end up on the shelf for a long time, or I have to eventually reduce the price. Pricing is still a tricky part of the business.

"I may never feel as though I'm being paid enough for my work, but I'm fortunate in being able to make a living at carving, and I don't ever take that for granted. I just have to be happy that I can keep doing what I'm doing, being creative and not getting bored at it, and continuing to be able to make a living doing something that I like."

DEALING WITH GALLERIES

Initially, you may sell most of your work at shows and through gift shops. As your work improves, galleries may be another option to explore. If you know an artist who has an established connection with a gallery, see if he or she will pave the way for your introduction to the gallery owner or manager. If you're going to approach a gallery on your own, do some research to make sure that it is reputable. If possible, visit the gallery before you contact its owner, scouting out the sort of work that's on display and evaluating whether your artwork will appeal to its market. If your carvings seem compatible with the gallery's offerings, find out the owner's name and its proper spelling, and send him or her a cover letter (ideally one page), along with your portfolio, or at least some high-quality photographs of your carvings (include retail prices). Indicate that you'd like to stop by at the gallery owner's or director's convenience to present some of your work for consideration. It's best to make an appointment beforehand, to avoid dropping in unexpectedly at an inconvenient time and to ensure that there's interest in your work before you pursue the lead any further.

Be on time for your appointment, and dress appropriately. What's appropriate will change depending on the gallery's location and clientele, as well as the owner's attitude. When you make your presentation, you'll be promoting yourself as well as your artwork. Your goal will be to demonstrate what's in it for them to add you to their roster of artists: How will your carvings appeal to their market and help further the gallery's interests and objectives? What aspects of your work will satisfy the needs and interests of the gallery's clientele? Along with your complete portfolio, also present two or three sample carvings.

Although the person you meet with may seem enthusiastic about your work, don't count on the deal until you're sure that everyone involved in the gallery's decision-making process is in on it. The gallery director, who handles sales, may appreciate your talent and want to represent you, but your style may not appeal to the gallery owner.

If your presentation went well and all decision makers are interested in your work, the next step is to negotiate an agreement. You may be able to sell your work to the gallery outright, leave your work on approval (for full or partial purchase within a specified period of time), or leave your carvings with the gallery on consignment, in which case you won't be paid until the work is sold.

Many galleries will accept work on consignment only, particularly when they're dealing with high-end pieces. Depending on the medium, galleries charge different sales commission rates for pieces on consignment. Sales commission rates can range from 33⅓ to 50 percent, with rates reportedly as high as 60 or 70 percent in some New York galleries. "Don't let the gallery tell you that you have to accept the sales commission rate they specify," says Dan Williams. "They may tell you that that's the rate for all of their artists, and it might be for most of the people they represent, but those numbers are always negotiable."

Many artists don't want to pay the high commissions and will not sell through galleries. But gallery owners and managers defend the fees for various reasons, including high overheads, which enable them to display your artwork in professional settings.

Floyd Scholz cites other disadvantages to dealing with galleries. "You rarely get to know the people who buy your work, which is very important. And sometimes galleries may demand exclusive rights on you as an artist, which means you won't be allowed to carve for anyone else."

Depending on your style and objectives, the costs of having a gallery represent you may be worth the benefits of having a middleman to help with distribution. If you're a talented wood sculptor, a reputable gallery will publicize your work, feature you in one-person shows, and sometimes get involved in pursuing commissions for you. "Galleries can be helpful if you're not particularly blessed with people skills; if not, let an agent or a gallery owner do it for you," says Floyd Scholz. "A lot of artists are not so good at selling their work—they're not good with money or discussing price—and that's why there are so many galleries. Most artists tend to be insecure about their work when a collector confronts them. Even some very famous bird carvers I know are incredibly insecure about what their work is worth."

"You need to look at a gallery from the standpoint that it's a team effort," says Leo Osborne. "They're part of the team and you're part of the team. Because you're the artist and the one who created the art doesn't mean that you're the only player on the team, unless you're just going to do your own selling. But if you're going to enlist the help of an agent, then you're involved in a partnership and you need to tread carefully. You can't go behind your partner's back, making sales to the gallery's clients and taking all the money and running. If you do, you'll probably do it only once, and then that's the end of that relationship. It's a very important relationship between the artists and the individual or gallery selling their work."

There are many reasons that it's important to be in a relationship with a reputable gallery, including the gallery's potential impact on your own reputation. For example, once the gallery pays you for a carving, its retail price is out of your control. Some self-employed carvers feel that this isn't a concern because they've already gotten their money out of the piece. But it could become a concern if what the gallery is charging for your work is way out of line with your own retail prices—on either the high or low side—or with the price of your work in nearby retail outlets.

"Right from the very beginning, I wholesaled my birds for half price," says Bob Guge. "The gallery owner said, 'You've got to wholesale them to me, so if people come to you, you've got to tell them twice the price because that's what I'll sell them for.' I sold them to him at my old price and doubled my price right on the spot. That was one of my biggest price increases, but it worked great. The gallery owner would take anything that I did, so I never had to worry about a sale. And if somebody came directly to me, it was like getting 100 percent profit."

To convince the gallery owner to purchase your work outright rather than on approval or on consignment, you have to be creative in your marketing, says Bill Veasey. "Tell the owner that if he or she buys something and it doesn't move in a certain amount of time, you'll trade it for something else." If you know who you're dealing with, or you've checked the gallery's credit rating, consider offering extended terms. This can be especially effective—crucial, even—if you're trying to sell to the owner of a gallery in a resort. If the gallery is doing its purchasing at the beginning of the season, you'll have a better shot at making the sale if you can extend terms of sixty or ninety days instead of thirty.

If the gallery can't afford to purchase your work outright, working on consignment can be advantageous. It might help you break into otherwise inaccessible high-end markets and give you a chance to prove the merits of your work to a gallery owner. If the gallery's clientele responds favorably to your carvings, you might develop a long-term, mutually profitable relationship with the gallery owner or director.

"Initially, consignment was the only opportunity we had, so that's what we did," says Dave Ahrendt. "It was just one of the ways we sold. We had a multifaceted marketing approach in which we also did shows and used other methods to market our work. We didn't want to sell all of our work through galleries, but we were willing to sell some. Selling your work through galleries can give you exposure and credibility. There are some things that you gain that don't show in your profit. Maybe you won't make as much if a gallery sells your work, but it's a way of showing people that you're credible. Galleries are more than just sales opportunities if they're the right kind of galleries."

However, some professionals who have spent years in the carving business caution against working on consignment. "I don't recommend consignment," says Bill Veasey. "You generally won't get top space in the store, unless you have a very powerful piece, and that means you're not going to get top consideration. If the owner has something he has bought outright, he'll try to turn his own money rather than yours. And every once in a while, an unscrupulous operator will steal a piece and then say he'll put in a claim. Most folks in business are honorable, but once in a while you'll encounter someone who's not. You can extend terms, but if you do, check the credit rating."

"You have to be very careful with galleries," says Phil Galatas. "You can send a piece to California, let's say, on consignment. You can price the piece at $10,000. The gallery might sell it for $15,000 but only give you a percentage of $10,000. And you won't know, because you're thousands of miles away. You have to keep up with it. You have to make sure you're dealing with a gallery you can trust."

There are some steps you can take to protect yourself against unscrupulous gallery owners. When you're leaving work on consignment, always ask for a detailed receipt, including a description of the artwork and its estimated value, or you won't have any proof to back up any subsequent claims. Find out whether the gallery carries insurance on work left on consignment. Verify the sales commission rate for pieces on consignment. If the gallery owner doesn't provide you with a contract, write a letter outlining your understanding of the terms of the agreement.

Your contract or letter should include a detailed description and the retail price of the carvings that you're leaving on consignment. Some artists stipulate that after a retail price for consignment pieces has been agreed upon, their work cannot be sold at a lower price without the carver's consent. Your letter should also specify the gallery's sales commission rate, including an indication of retail price and what you will net; the extent of exclusivity; the length of time that the gallery will act as your sales representative; the terms of payment (for example, within fifteen days of the sale of your work and/or regularly once a month); and commercial use of art and reproduction rights.

DEALING WITH COLLECTORS

As you build your reputation and your work becomes better known, you'll have to increasingly deal with collectors as well as gift shop and gallery owners. Negotiations with collectors will take many forms. For instance, you may have already completed a piece that just won a top award at the World Championship, and a carving aficionado may have expressed interest in adding your award-winning piece to his or her collection. On the other hand, someone may have just discovered your style and would like to commission you to create a large wood sculpture for his or her foyer, so you'll have to work out the artistic and business details in advance.

If approached strategically, shows like the Southeastern Wildlife Exposition offer a good opportunity to line up future commissions. "Before you go to a show, you should be thinking about everything you're going to do over the next year," says Pat Godin. "Have an idea of the concept of the carving and what you want to communicate with it," so that if someone expresses interest in commissioning your work, you can pitch your idea. "The ideal thing would be for the collector to tell you that he or she wants to buy it. Generally I'll give collectors a range of where I think the carving will fall in price, especially the more expensive pieces, which are sometimes hard to price. If you've thought about your work ahead of time, it's a big advantage at a show."

Before you finalize the carving's price and promise delivery by a certain date, make sure you thoroughly understand what the customer has in mind. To prevent future misunderstandings, make sure both you and the collector have the same idea before you begin the carving. Some master carvers create a small clay model to clarify their impression of what the collector is seeking. Others rough out a sketch.

"When someone is interested in commissioning you to carve a particular type of bird, offer to do a little sketch at no charge," says Eldridge Arnold. "If the customer likes it, then you can haggle over a price. Once that's agreed upon, send a letter with a copy of the sketch, and request one-third of the total cost up front. Halfway through the project, request another third. And after the project's done, the remainder. This is very important because once you've got one-third of the money, you seldom end up with a situation at the end in which the person says he or she doesn't like the piece. But if you don't get paid up front or as you go along, the person has an advantage on you and can say, 'That's not what I expected.' And without having done a sketch or clay model at the beginning, you don't have a leg to stand on.

"Another way to protect yourself is through the use of a contract, although I've never used one. I send photos every two or three weeks and continue sending photos of works in progress so that my customers can see the progression of the work all the way through. And they love it. They're involved and know where their money is going. It also would let me know if there were any complaints along the way, although that's never happened."

Establish the terms of your agreement up front. Along with the artistic specifications, your letter or contract should include the carving's price, delivery date, and terms of payment.

If a person is seriously interested in your work but can't afford to pay off the balance when the commissioned piece is complete, if you know the collector or can check his or her credit rating, you can offer the option of installment payments. "My willingness to offer a flexible payment plan has salvaged a couple of major sales that I otherwise would have lost," says Floyd Scholz.

If a collector balks at the price of a carving that you've already completed, you might share some details about your creative process. "The question of how long it takes comes up only if a collector asks why a piece is so expensive," says Scholz. "Then I'll say, 'Well, I spent five months on this piece. When you break that down, it's not that much money per week that I'm earning.' I suppose you could scare someone off with too high a price. But instead of scaring them off, give them alternatives. Say, well, I understand that that might be a bit out of your range, but I also do miniatures, or I also do birds with a little bit less detail. To really make a living at this, you have to be flexible."

Scholz advises that you be consistent in your pricing no matter who the buyer is. "Don't tell one guy, just because he drives up in a Mercedes, that you want $30,000 for a hawk carving, and then another collector who shows up in a Geo Metro that he can have it for $15,000, because eventually the first collector will find out," Scholz says.

"When discussing price, the most important thing is to exude confidence without being arrogant. Look the collector right in the eye and make him believe that he is getting the absolute best deal on the planet. When someone asks you how much a bird costs, say, 'It's $50,000,' not, 'Well, I dunno, would you give me $50,000?' You've got to be very confident and matter-of-fact about it. When you start stuttering and becoming hesitant, the collector will think that you're not really sure and he's got to be careful because he doesn't want to be taken for a ride."

Although commissions can be lucrative, they seem like double-edged swords to some master carvers. They let the carvers keep doing what they want to do, but not always the way, or at the time, they want to do it. "At this point, I work primarily on commission," says Larry Barth. "I don't like it, but that's the case. I vastly preferred the earlier days, when I carved what I wanted to carve, and when it was done, I put it up for sale. But now I'm dealing with banks and mortgages and supporting a family, and I need a little more stability than carving on speculation gave me. When working on commission, I know where each piece I work on is going before I start."

INSURANCE

Check your homeowner's policy to see if a home business is specifically excluded by your insurance company. This is the case with many insurance companies, and they will not cover the home for damages, whether or not the damages are related to the business, if they find out that you were operating a home business without their knowledge. Personal liability and medical emergencies are everyday risks that you need to insure yourself against.

When you're about to make the leap to carving on a full-time basis, talk to your insurance agent about your plans, and have the agent write a rider to your homeowner's policy if possible. The rider should be relatively inexpensive for your one-person home business and may be well worth any extra expense. The agent will want to know how much coverage you wish to purchase. This will require you to assess the value of your tools, equipment, inventory, vehicle, and finished carvings. Take the agent's advice regarding adequate liability insurance coverage, or consult with an attorney.

The company carrying your homeowner's policy may decide not to issue you a rider. In this case, you will need to take out a business owner's policy. This is especially important if you plan to open your own gallery or expect customers in your shop. The business policy can be tailored to your specific needs, and you may be able to reduce the premiums by installing burglar alarms and improving the general safety of the premises by installing appropriate guards on power tools.

You probably already have motor vehicle insurance. But do you carry enough coverage? Money may be tight while you are in the start-up phase of your business, and the financial consequences of an automobile accident could be devastating. If you use your vehicle for business purposes, find out if your policy covers you in the event of a business-related accident. As in the case of the homeowner's policy, you may need to acquire a rider to your auto insurance policy that will cover your business use or business travel.

TAX CONSIDERATIONS

Don't wait to think about taxes until they're due. Ask your accountant or tax advisor for hints on how to keep detailed, accurate books and how you can benefit from some of the tax advantages for self-employed individuals. If you're at least somewhat familiar with the tax code, it will help you make smarter decisions in your purchasing, pricing, selling, and the overall way that you operate your business.

Save *all* business-related receipts, such as those for magazine subscriptions, exhibit fees, phone calls, postage, and shipping, and keep thorough records. If each receipt doesn't spell it out clearly, record the purpose of the expenditures on the receipt. File your receipts regularly, or at least periodically, to save yourself frustration at tax time. It can sometimes be difficult to remember what you did in July of the previous year as you're getting your tax information together in March.

During 1996 the U.S. Congress enacted a considerable number of tax code changes, which went into effect in 1997. Some of the tax advantages available to the self-employed are described below, but since these suggestions are not exhaustive, you should consult a professional for current and comprehensive details.

The money that you spend on equipment in your start-up may be deductible in the first year. This is known as *business expensing* and may include carving tools, business equipment, and any other non-real estate assets that you put into service in the first year. This write-off can take the place of calculating depreciation on the equipment over a period of years. The write-off cannot exceed the income for the year, although any excess amount can be carried over to the next year. See section 179 of the Internal Revenue Code for details on first-year write-offs.

If you're the sole proprietor of your home business, you will be subject to self-employment taxes. If the income from the sale of your carvings and other product lines is substantial, you have to remember to set aside some of this income for the IRS, state income tax, and self-employment tax.

If your business is not just a part-time effort, you are probably eligible for the Self-Employed Health Insurance Deduction.

Vehicle expenses can be deducted as actual expenses or at a standard rate per business-related mile. If you prefer to deduct actual expenses, you need to save all of your receipts, including those for tolls, parking, maintenance, and repairs. The actual deduction is based on the ratio of business miles to total miles, so throughout the year, record mileage whenever you use your vehicle. Make it a habit to record whether each trip—even a short trip around town—was for business or other purposes. You may also be able to claim vehicle depreciation if you use your vehicle extensively for business purposes.

Business trips can be written off fully only if the primary purpose of the trip was related to carving, such as attendance at a show or competition. If you cannot meet this simple test, you should not claim the full deduction. If a portion of travel was relevant to business interests, you may be able to deduct a portion of your hotel bill and meals, but keep careful records in case your deduction is questioned. If your business is set up so that your spouse is an employee, you can write off his or her expenses as well.

The in-home office or shop deduction (square footage percentage) is allowed if you spend most of your working time and conduct the most important part of your work there. Recent rulings make it difficult for part-time home office or shop owners to take advantage of this deduction. Consult with your tax accountant to see if you qualify.

INTERNET SITES

To help you keep up with changes in the tax code and other financial aspects of running your own business, you can search small business or home business-related Web sites on the Internet. You can find relevant Web sites by going to search engines such as Webcrawler, Yahoo, Excite, or Lycos. After the search engine is up, select "business," then "small business" or "home business," and browse through the wealth of information that's out there. Some of the advice may be promotional or not thoroughly tested, however, so critically evaluate the source of the information and scrutinize the material with a critical eye.

❖ CHAPTER 7 ❖

The Carving Life

Geese appear high over us,
pass, and the sky closes. Abandon,
as in love or sleep, holds
them to their way, clear
in the ancient faith: what we need
is here. And we pray, not
for new earth or heaven, but to be
quiet in heart, and in eye
clear. What we need is here.
                    —Wendell Berry, *"The Wild Geese"*

By now you realize that there are trade-offs in the life of the professional carver. With dedication and commitment, you can achieve the sort of creative lifestyle you may have dreamed of. But you have to be willing to work hard, consistently, and to make some sacrifices. If new cars, large homes, and expensive vacations are more important to you than the freedom to create your own schedule while pursuing what you love, you should consider seeking a different kind of employment.

For the most part, you can plan your own calendar, although you may sometimes have to cater to the constraints of teaching or shows. And you'll get to decide how you're going to spend most of your days. You'll be free to tackle your most challenging work during the hours in the day when you're most productive. But that freedom will require self-direction plus an ability to set and consistently work toward your goals. When you encounter obstacles, you'll need to sustain your energy and enthusiasm. And as self-employed carvers repeatedly emphasize, you'll need enough self-discipline to apply the seat of your pants to the seat of your chair when you have to meet a deadline.

"I like working for me," says Rosalyn Leach Daisey. "I like having control over my own life. I like deciding what I'm going to do each day. If I wake up and want to traipse around in the marsh with duck boots and a camera and mosquito repellent, or go visit my publisher or another carver, the decision's mine. I work ten to twelve hours a day, and when I go down to the shop in the morning, I ask myself what I feel like doing that day? Carving and getting dirty? Texturing or painting? Whatever I feel like doing, I do. By the end of the day, I want to have such and such accomplished. I set goals every day but seldom start a piece and work all the way through on it. And that way I can do what I feel like doing. Therein lies the secret, because creativity is fostered when there are no restrictions."

Although entrepreneurs tend to work more than play, some prevent burnout by scheduling downtime, at least occasionally. Even a brief vacation from carving and a change of perspective will likely improve your productivity. "You'll never have a paid vacation, but your time is your own," says Bart Walter. "And if you want to take a day off because the sun is shining and birds are singing, it's perfectly fine. You're not going to earn any income while you're doing that, but since you don't know what your income is going to be at the end of the year, it's neither in the plus column nor in the minus column. Sometimes I won't let myself take the day off, but I try to take advantage of this flexibility as often as possible. Life's too short to do nothing but work. And when you take the day off to go canoeing and studying birds, let's face it, you're still working, but you're having fun.

"I spent a week in Florida one winter between exhibitions, and I didn't have anything to do, so I went to Ding Darling National

Wildlife Refuge. I paddled around in my canoe and used my binoculars and sketch pad, and I sketched about five hours a day. It felt like a vacation, even though I was working. But it wasn't work for me; it was fun. And that is how I would choose to spend my vacation—studying birds and animals. That's my idea of a good time."

"I work hard, and then I play hard," says Larry Barth. "The whole trick to being self-employed is the discipline. To me, a day breaks down into three segments—morning, afternoon, and evening—and I try to work two of the three. That's the nice thing about being self-employed: I get to decide which two. And you can make up the time. If you don't work at all one day, then you owe two thirds. And that's when things are just cruising along nicely, which doesn't often happen.

"When you start working hard for a deadline, you're working all three thirds. And sometimes you're working four thirds. So it varies. I've never been able to decide whether I work better under pressure or that's just when I work. But I definitely put in more hours when there's a deadline, and anymore it seems like there's a deadline constantly. So it's pretty all-consuming.

"I end up working around the clock for about a week before a deadline. I hate it, but that's what I end up doing all the time. And this is the whole paradox for me. It's no way to live, but it's the best way to get work done. Because when you're working at something that intensively, you're so in tune with it that everything just flows. It's a very efficient way to work but a terrible way to live. So you've got to strike a balance. Because the best way to carve birds is to go in there and never stop until it's done. You don't lose any momentum shifting gears. You don't have to warm up again the next day. These things already take too long, and if you start taking too many breaks, then they take forever.

"I can get a whole lot done real fast if I get into 'the zone,' so to speak, and don't even come up for air. I just start working around the clock and drop everything else around me. I don't drive a car. I don't go into town. I don't do anything else. I'm in my shop working hard, and my family's gotten used to that, and they know not to bug me when the push is on. Even when I'm working hard like that, I still need breaks, so I'll spend twenty minutes or so playing football with my son, and that feels real good. A change of pace is as good as a night's sleep sometimes."

Many self-employed carvers emphasize the benefits of some sort of physical recreation every day. Whether you take a hike through the woods or a walk through a city park, you're recharging your batteries. "As a carver you spend a lot of time sitting and concentrating, and you have to balance that with physical training too," says Floyd Scholz, who takes a daily 4-mile hike whenever possible. "In athletic training, you learn how to care for yourself and your body. I could not do what I do today at the same level and intensity without a foundation of athletic training. I learned to pace myself. And I learned what my capabilities are. You have to know your limits."

The pressure of the annual World Championship compels many master carvers to sweat it right down to the deadline. "The time leading up to the World Championship is the worst time in my life," says Jett Brunet. "I hate it. Having to be on a deadline like that makes me dislike carving. My goal is always to do my best. That's what I strive for. But when there's a deadline, you have to do your best in a limited period of time. So you're struggling with having to do better work than you've ever done before, but you only have so much time to do it in. And those things work against each other.

"When you're on a deadline, your only chance to do your best work is by working longer hours. So you start working longer days. Your judgment is kind of off, and you see things that aren't there when you're not sleeping much. I used to do that for every show, but now I only do it for the World Championship.

"Since my goal is to always do my best work, I would never get anything finished without a deadline. I think Bob Guge once said, 'A bird takes as much time as you have.' So you're working and working as the deadline approaches, and the greatest feeling in the world is the day that you decide the bird is done—the day the show is here. When the World Championship is finally here, and the bird is done (and somehow you always get it done), the joy of that feeling is as powerful as the depressing feeling that you had the night before. When you enter and it wins, all of your struggling and everything you put yourself through to get it done makes the feeling more intense. It's crazy, and we wonder why we do it. But a lot of income has to do with pushing to finish your bird."

In most competitions, but particularly the World, even the pros get discouraged when their birds don't get the recognition they might deserve. "If you're really into competitions and you spend all your time on what you think is a great bird and someone else doesn't, that's a bummer," says Bob Guge. "I learned a long time ago, and especially when I started judging, that nobody's perfect. Everybody make mistakes. I don't know everything, and no one else does either. Subconsciously, you make decisions as a judge, and you miss things. I've learned that I've got to compete against myself, and if I'm happy with something, I need to be satisfied with that. If I'm not, then I should accept what's going to happen instead of worrying about why the judges picked someone else's bird. That's something you have to get over."

"A lot of people get caught up in the competitions and winning prizes," says Bart Walter. "If what you want to do happens to be the same as what's winning prizes, by all means do it. But if what you want to do is one thing and what's winning is another, don't change your style to fit what you think the judges might want. The judges are just a set of people who are making a decision that day. Next year it may be a different set of judges, and they'll have a different set of barometers. Instead of carving or sculpting for someone else, you have to do it for yourself. Otherwise, there isn't much point in doing it, and you should go get a real job, one that will bring in a steady income."

When you have an outside job with either a large or small company, chances are that your day is full of social connections, such as chatting with a coworker on the production line or rehashing last night's game with a friend during a coffee break. But as an artist working at home day after day, you may feel somewhat isolated. If you tend to enjoy interacting with others, you may be challenged by the solitude that carving sometimes requires. "It's a very lonely way to make a living, because you're working alone," says Floyd Scholz. "I sit here by myself. Yes, I have a secretary now and a guy who works for me who's sort of a handyman, but when I'm here carving my birds, I'm here by myself. I work alone. You have to, unless you're a husband-and-wife team, but even then, it's a very lonely way to make a living."

Some master carvers enjoy the solitude of carving but equally enjoy the camaraderie at shows and competitions. Though competitors are sometimes vying for the same ribbons, many carvers return to the World Championship year after year for its professional benefits and a sense of community with their peers. And in between competitions, some carvers maintain their connections by daily on-line conversations via E-mail and the Woodcarver Mailing List (see chapter 3).

As a professional carver, you can also enjoy social benefits beyond the community of carvers. "You get to meet fascinating people just going to art shows, for instance," says Bart Walter. "You get to take advantage of some of the perks of being a professional artist. You get to travel between social circles. You're neither white collar nor blue collar. I can show up at a party terribly overdressed or terribly underdressed and nobody really gives a darn. They just shake their heads and say, well, he's an artist. So I just don't sweat it, usually, unless there's a major client there. I have no reason to sweat it, because people expect artists to be a bit different, so have fun with that."

When you operate a home-based business, it's sometimes difficult to convey to your neighbors, students, and even your family that you're working. If a neighbor drops in for conversation or a student stops by for technical advice when you're working on a piece that requires concentration, you'll have to tactfully make it clear that you don't have time to socialize. If people don't seem to get the message, you may have to be abrupt, maybe almost rude, to establish boundaries.

"People come around to visit and to see if I want to go fishing, and it's difficult getting them to understand that I have to work," says Jett Brunet. "Especially when a big deadline is ahead of me, I try to give my total focus to what I'm doing. When I'm in what I call my 'World mode,' from February to April as the World Championship nears, I shut down most of my outside life, except on weekends.

From Monday through Friday, I try to stay focused and to have as few distractions as possible. So I end up intensely working on a particular decoy. When I tell friends that I can't go fishing, it's not so much taking the time to go fishing or losing the half of a day that's the problem; it's the time that it would take me to get back into my work. When I'm trying to do World-quality work for the World Championship competitions, it's difficult to get focused. It seems like there are a lot of distractions. And the week before the show, when you seem to need the time to concentrate the most, that's when other carvers are calling to see what you're doing and when you'll get there. When you most need to focus, that's when you get the most distractions."

Even when you're not gearing up for competition, no matter how well you've established social boundaries, there will be interruptions in your day. You may get a call from the school nurse when your child gets sick at school. And since you're the one at home all day, you'll likely have to deal with routine as well as unexpected household maintenance. The ability to manage your time will give you an edge in handling unforeseen events, but you'll still lose productivity.

"When something happens, if you've got to take a kid to the hospital or whatever, then that means you have to work twice as hard the next day or make up the time the next night when you should be sleeping. It's also tough when the kids are here," says Bob Guge, who has eight children. "With my workshop right here at the house, there's always somebody who needs something, always a fight to break up. But the kids will all be gone someday, and I won't have to worry about that."

Along with your artistic concerns, as the owner of your own business, your administrative responsibilities will include bookkeeping, planning, ordering, shipping, pricing, and customer and public relations. You may often find yourself simultaneously completing an intricate carving, negotiating your next commission, and lining up another project to follow. Even when things in your business are rolling along smoothly, you should regularly devote some time to marketing your work and to taking advantage of promotional opportunities as they arise.

"You start running a business and it's tough," says Bob Guge. "My father helps me on some things. My brother works for me part-time and does all the band saw work and sanding on my primitives. I still carve them and paint them, but he does all the busywork. These things help make it possible for me to do what I do best, which is to carve birds. But in many cases, I've declined retail sales of my casts. I'll sell something once in a while at a class, but I don't advertise the casts because I just couldn't afford packing one or two birds here to sell them. The money wouldn't be worth the time I'd lose from what I can do best.

"I'm a better carver than I am at handling the business aspects and doing those other logistical things, but unfortunately, you have to do it. If you just carve a few birds a year, there's nothing to it. But because I sell a lot of primitives and also have a line of reproductions that I sell all over the country, there's a lot of wholesaling and book work. These things all make it possible to be a carver full-time, but they also keep me from carving. And between my birds and my work and my teaching, there's no time left. It's nice to be your own boss, but no one's going to do your work for you."

After fourteen years of earning their living as full-time carvers, Dave and Mary Ahrendt grew tired of the constraints imposed by relying on carving as their sole source of income. In 1996 they had the opportunity to purchase a summer resort, the fulfillment of a long-time dream. They operate the resort for six months out of the year and pursue their art from November through April.

"It gives us a bit of financial freedom, in the sense that we're no longer totally dependent on having to sell our carvings," says Dave. "As long as we've been carving, we've had to sell our carvings to make a living. In order to survive as a family, we needed that income from our carving." But as they head into the next phase of their lives, the Ahrendts hope that the economic freedom that running the resort gives them will allow them to spend more time carving what they want to carve, and not just what they feel will sell.

As a full-time carver, your financial situation may be shaky at times, and you'll have to learn to live with fluctuations in cash flow.

Although you may not get wealthy in conventional terms, you'll derive satisfaction from what you create. And unlike those who work primarily with intangibles, you'll have the benefit of seeing what you've produced and enjoying its effect on others.

"You're not going to get rich doing this," says Bart Walter. "There are some people who make good money at it, but it's very difficult to do, unless you're just a born marketer as well as being skilled. Money is not the most important thing in this world, and if you think it is, you should probably not pursue art as a career. Go do something where you are guaranteed a paycheck and where the chances are that you'll earn a lot more money. You might do quite well financially in bird carving or sculpture or painting, but chances are you'll just get by—if you're lucky. If you're carving just to make money, you're probably not producing very good carvings. Carve because you love it, and then you'll have a chance of producing something significant, something good, something meaningful."

The artistic aspects of carving are most important to Larry Barth. "I don't care so much about money as I do about pursuing art," he says. "But making money is a necessary evil that goes hand in hand with it. If you don't make money, you cease to make a living, and then you can't keep doing what you want to do. I can't make as much money as some people because I'm not willing to compromise. I take each piece as far as I can take it.

"I'm a terrible businessman. I don't think that I've succeeded because of my business sense, but on the merit of my work. My family is willing to live with the erratic income and the long dry spells that go with this lifestyle. I'm really fortunate that it has all worked out. I don't enjoy the business side of bird carving at all, but I do view it as something that has to be done. Linda takes care of finances and does the taxes. And she tries to help me with correspondence, but there are a lot of times that she just can't do it. I'm the one who has to write the letters and get the stuff out."

But there *are* some financial perks for a full-time carver. "You can do all sorts of things and use them as tax deductions because you're watching birds everywhere you go," says Bart Walter. "And if you're a professional and you're seriously committed, chances are that you're watching birds everywhere you go. It just becomes a habit. It's not something you even think about, but chances are that you're watching birds while you're driving down the highway. You're looking for hawks on the roadside. It's just one of those quirks.

"You get to travel, do interesting things, and see interesting places. And then there's the research end of it. There are birds all around the world. If you can get there, there are birds there. And that's a special gift. You go to Florida for an exhibition, and there's a tremendous variety of birds, even in the city when you go to a museum."

"I just love to carve birds," Bob Guge says. "I think the Lord blessed me with a talent, and this is what I like to do. I get up every morning wanting to carve birds. Sometimes it's hard, when you have to do it. But you've got to work, and it's good if you can do something you like and make money at it. I like teaching, and I just love doing birds. It's neat to step back and look at what you've created.

"Probably the biggest pitfall in the life of a carver is when you finish a piece and it's not what you wanted it to be. There have been times when I've worked hard on a bird, and the person who was going to buy it or who it was done for wasn't excited about it. That's probably the biggest bummer. It's happened to me a few times. But then there have been other times when I've seen the opposite reaction. I started a bird in a class, and it just had all the charisma in the world. And the guy I did it for loved it, and two other people wanted it too. It just had that life essence in it."

Larry Barth, who lives with his wife Linda and two children in the mountains of western Pennsylvania, builds his whole life around his art. When he's not in his studio, he's usually somewhere sketching, bird-watching, or walking in the woods. "It's a full-time thing, and I don't resent being 'on call,' so to speak, around the clock, because I'm doing what I want," he says.

"I am as content as can be in my current situation. We've lived here for a little over a dozen years, and I've built a studio separate from the house. And I'm in my studio right now and I'm looking out the window, and I've got a trout stream rolling right past my deck. I can feed brook trout from my deck. I've got bears and turkeys and pileated woodpeckers and a barn owl, and there's a wood duck nesting right outside my studio window. This is perfect, and this time of year, I've got wildflowers galore. I can hardly get any work done because I've just got to walk around and reacquaint myself with all my wildflower friends. I feel so good about just being here and working.

"What I do is simply my response to the beauty I see in nature, specifically birds and the things that go with them. I see something that's just so riveting that I'm compelled to return to my studio to try to create what I've seen. That act of creation is a celebration of that beauty. It's my attempt to capture and hold it. When I make a bird, I come to possess it in a way. And carving a bird that has inspired me is my way of capturing and holding and possessing that moment—to communicate it to others."

Appendix

DAVE AND MARY AHRENDT
Park Rapids, Minnesota
Years as professionals: 14
Age they started woodcarving: 25
Artistic mediums: Oil paint, wood (Mary also uses watercolors).
Competitive awards: Ward Foundation World Championship—Open Class Interpretive, 1992 First Place; five times Birds in Art at Leigh Yawkey Woodson Art Museum (1988, 1989, 1990, 1991, 1996).
Most significant professional achievement: "Supporting a family for 13 years with carving as our sole source of income."

ELDRIDGE ARNOLD
Greenwich, Connecticut
Years as a professional: 22
Age he started woodcarving: 48
Artistic mediums: Acrylic, oil and watercolor; tupelo gum and basswood; brass and sheet metal.
Competitive awards: Ward Foundation World Championship—1982 Best in Show; 1981 Second Best in Show; 1980 Best in Confidence Class; Pacific Flyway Show—1978 Best in Show; 1979 California Open; many other Best in Shows and First, Second and Third Places.
Most significant professional achievement: "It has been extremely rewarding for me to be able to practice in the field that I was trained in. I'm grateful for access to the Ward Foundation's many wonderful exhibitions over the years. The Bruce Museum in Greenwich, Connecticut, provided me with a great honor by asking me to exhibit in their new museum in 1994."

LARRY BARTH
Stahlstown, Pennsylvania
Years as a professional: 25
Age he started woodcarving: 14
Artistic mediums: Wood, clay, illustration.
Competitive awards: Ward Foundation World Championship—1984 Best in Show Lifesize Open, Best in Show Miniature Open; 1985 Best in World Lifesize; 1986 Best in World Lifesize; 1991 Best in World Lifesize; 1993 Best in World Lifesize; 1997 Best in World Lifesize; 1979, 1987, 1990 Second Best in World.
Most significant professional achievement: Selection as the 1991 Leigh Yawkey Woodson Master Wildlife Artist.

BOB BOOTH (Native Born Carvings)
Modest Town, Virginia
Years as a professional: 15
Age he started woodcarving: early 30s
Artistic mediums: Acrylic and milk paints, wood.
Competitive awards: Quite a few ribbons in early years, then changed to folk art style (not many competitions have these as a category).
Most significant professional achievement: Placed first for three consecutive years at Chincoteague Show for Head Carving. (Competed one time in Ward Foundation World Championships—placed sixth in 1972.)

JETT BRUNET
Galliano, Louisiana
Years as a professional: 15
Age he started woodcarving: 9
Artistic mediums: Tupelo; oils and acrylic.
Competitive awards: Ward Foundation World Championship—1985 and 1987 (World Pairs); two-time most outstanding teenage carver at the World. Best of Show awards at every level at World Show (Novice, Intermediate, Open, World). Only carver to win first, second, and third Best of Show open floating decoys, World Show; seven Best of Shows, Open Floating, World Show the last five in a row. Won Best of Show in three different categories at the 1993 PFDA show.
Most significant professional achievement: Five Best of Shows in a row (Open Floating World Show).

TAN BRUNET
Galliano, Louisiana
Years as a professional: 40
Age he started woodcarving: 12
Artistic mediums: Oils on wood and canvas.
Competitive awards: Ward Foundation World Championship—five Best in World; two Best of Show (World); first Master Carver, Hall of Fame; many Best of Shows coast-to-coast; 12 Head Whittling Championships (1977, 1978, 1981, 1982, 1983 Best in World Pairs); 1984, 1985 Best of Show, World (Floating Decoys).
Most significant professional achievement: Best in World five times.

JO CRAEMER
Georgetown, Delaware
Years as a professional carver: 13
Age she started woodcarving: 42
Artistic mediums: Wood, occasionally clay.
Competitive awards: Assorted ribbons at various competitions ranging from honorable mention to first place.
Most significant professional achievement: Being asked to teach workshops and seminars at the Ward Foundation.

ROSALYN LEACH DAISEY
Newark, Delaware
Years as a professional: 18
Age she started woodcarving: 34
Artistic mediums: Wood and acrylic.
Competitive awards: Ward Foundation World Championship— Best of Shows at the U.S. National Competition on Long Island, NY; Mid-Atlantic Wildfowl Competition in Virginia Beach, VA; and the Garden State Wildfowl Competition, Red Bank, NJ.
Most significant professional achievement: Having my fifth hardcover carving text published by Schiffer Publishing.

GEORGIA F. DAYHOFF
Colorado Springs, Colorado
Years as a professional: 15
Age she started woodcarving: 55
Artistic mediums: Woods, basswood, walnut, and tupelo; copper acrylic.
Competitive awards: Many from Colorado Carvers' Shows; Cheyenne Mountain Zoo Art Show; Cook Communications Ministeries Art Show; Palmer Lake Art Show.
Most significant professional achievement: Getting the commission to carve 12 birds for the Garden of the Gods Visitors' Center in Colorado Springs, Colorado.

PHIL GALATAS
Humboldt, Nebraska
Years as a professional: 20
Age he started woodcarving: 27
Artistic mediums: Oil and acrylic; wood, canvas, metal.
Competitive awards: Ward Foundation World Championship—1987, 1989, 1992 Gulf South Champion Decorative Lifesize; 1989, 1990 World Champion Decorative Miniature.
Most significant professional achievement: Second time winning a World Championship; exhibiting at National Geographic headquarters in Washington, D.C.

PAT GODIN
Paris, Ontario, Canada
Years as a professional: 18
Age he started woodcarving: 14
Artistic mediums: Acrylic paint, three-dimensional, wood, steel, bronze.
Competitive awards: Ward Foundation World Championship—1976, 1980, 1984 World Champion Decorative Decoy Pairs; 1982, 1995 Decorative Lifesize.
Most significant professional achievement: Being inducted into 1994 Easton Waterfowl Festival Hall of Fame; publishing three instructional books.

BOB GUGE
Sleepy Hollow, Illinois
Years as a professional: 18
Age he started woodcarving: 18
Artistic mediums: Acrylic; tupelo, jelutong, and basswood.
Competitive awards: Ward Foundation World Championship—
1984, 1988, 1989, 1991 Best in World Decorative Miniature; numerous other Best of Shows at competitions such as Northern National Championship and U.S. National Carving Contest.
Most significant professional achievement: Numerous years of exhibiting in Leigh Yawkey Woodson Art Museum's Birds in Art exhibition.

W.F. (BILL) JUDT
Grand Prairie, Alberta, Canada
Years as a professional: 22
Age he started woodcarving: 25
Artistic mediums: Relief woodcarving.
Competitive awards: (Does not compete.)
Most significant professional achievement: Establishing on-line woodcarving with woodcarver mailing list and woodcarver e-zine at wwwoodcarver.com. Publishing his first book, *Relief Carving Treasury.*

ERNIE MUEHLMATT
Salisbury, Maryland
Years as a professional: 30
Age he started woodcarving: 40
Artistic mediums: Wood.
Competitive awards: Ward Foundation World Championship—
three times World Champion (1979, 1981, 1984); many Best of Shows in Open Division.
Most significant professional achievement: Induction into Carvers' Hall of Fame at Easton Waterfowl Festival.

LEO E. OSBORNE
Guemes Island, Anacortes, Washington
Years as a professional: 25
Age he started woodcarving: late 20s
Artistic mediums: Wood, bronze, stone, and paint on canvas.
Competitive awards: Seven awards of excellence, Society of Animal Artists; four Don Miller Awards for Interpretive Sculpture; Margaret Hexter Prize, National Sculpture Society; numerous Best of Show Awards at many wildlife expositions; First, Second, and Third Place awards at the Ward Foundation World Championship.
Most significant professional achievement: Eleven years of exhibiting at Birds in Art, Leigh Yawkey Woodson Art Museum.

FLOYD SCHOLZ
Hancock, Vermont
Years as a professional: 15
Age he started woodcarving: 10
Artistic mediums: Wood and acrylics.
Competitive awards: Ward Foundation World Championship—1989 Third in World; 1992 Second in World; 28 Best in Shows; numerous other awards throughout the country.
Most significant professional achievement: Writing *Birds of Prey*, Stackpole's bestselling book on raptors.

JIM SPRANKLE
Sanibel Island, Florida
Years as a professional carver: 27
Age he started woodcarving: 28
Artistic mediums: Wood and acrylics.
Competitive awards: Ward Foundation World Championship—several
Most significant professional achievement: Being elected to Waterfowl Festival, first year of eligibility.

PATI STAJCAR
Golden, Colorado
Years as a professional: 12
Age she started woodcarving: 22
Artistic mediums: Wood, marble, bronze.
Competitive awards: Ward Foundation World Championship—1990 and 1997 Third in World; numerous First Place and Best of Show Awards.
Most significant professional achievement: "It was at a tiny little show in Manitou Springs, Colorado, only 40 artists, but the artists voted my work the best of show—that meant the most to me. Professionally, the 1995 National Sculpture Society, Pietro and Alfrieda Montana Memorial Award."

WILLIAM VEASEY
Newark, Delaware
Years as a professional: 25
Age he started woodcarving: 39
Artistic mediums: Wood, canvas.
Competitive awards: Ward Foundation World Championship—several Best in Show awards, including Hunting Decoy contests, head carving contests, painting contests, etc.
Most significant professional achievement: Contributing to the literature in the field and arranging for others to do the same. Induction into Easton Waterfowl Festival Hall of Fame.

BART WALTER
Westminster, Maryland
Years as a professional: 11
(Number of years as a professional sculptor: 17)
Age he started woodcarving: 14
Artistic mediums: Bronze
Competitive awards: Ward Foundation World Championship—1986 Professional/Open Class Best in Show.
Most significant professional achievement: One-man exhibition (32 sculptures, 22 drawings) at the A. G. Poulain Municipal Museum in Vernon, France, 1996.

DAN WILLIAMS
Owings Mills, Maryland
Years as a professional: 20
Age he started woodcarving: Teens; seriously at 29
Artistic mediums: Woodcarving, photography.
Competitive awards: Ward Foundation World Championship—250 Blue in national competitions, 37 Best of Shows; National Shorebird Championship; Southeastern Wildlife Exposition Champion two years in a row.
Most significant professional achievement: Being the featured carver at Easton Waterfowl Festival and Southeastern Wildlife Exposition in the same year.

GREG WOODARD
Brigham, Utah
Years as a professional: 10
Age he started woodcarving: 25
Artistic mediums: Tupelo, oil paint.
Competitive awards: Ward Foundation World Championship—1992 World Class/Lifesize Decorative Best in World; four Best of Shows at World; three North American Best of Shows; numerous Best of Shows, California Open.
Most significant professional achievement: Winning the World Class in 1992.

❖ SELECTED EVENTS ❖

February
Southeastern Wildlife
    Exposition
211 Meeting Street
Charleston, SC 29401
(803) 723-1748

April
Ward World Championship
    Wildfowl Carving
    Competition
The Ward Foundation
909 S. Schumaker Drive
Salisbury, MD 21801
(410) 742-4988

August
Sculpture in the Park
Loveland Sculpture Invitational
P.O. Box 7006
Loveland, CO 80537
(800) 551-1752 or (970) 663-
    7467

September
Birds in Art
Leigh Yawkey Woodson Art
    Museum
700 N. Twelfth Street
Wausau, WI 54403
(715) 845-7010

November
Easton Waterfowl Festival
P.O. Box 929
Easton, MD 21601
(410) 822-4567

❖ BIBLIOGRAPHY ❖

Kotler, Philip, and Gary Armstrong. *Principles of Marketing*. Englewood Cliffs, N.J.: Prentice Hall, 1991.

Lasser, J.K. *Your Income Tax 1998*. New York: Simon and Schuster, 1997.

Levinson, Jay Conrad, and Seth Godin. *Guerrilla Marketing for the Home-based business*. New York: Houghton Mifflin, 1995.

Nickerson, Clarence B. *Accounting Handbook for Nonaccountants*. New York: Van Nostrand Reinhold, 1986.

Ries, Al, and Jack Trout. *Positioning: The Battle for Your Mind*. New York: McGraw-Hill, 1986.

❖ INDEX ❖